MW01268494

A way

AT A CAMP IN MAINE

Kimberley Collins Kalicky

ISBN: 1451562292
ISBN-13: 9781451562293

Dedicated to

Harold and Eileen

Sarah

TABLE OF CONTENTS

CHAPTER 1

Return

Stepping out of our car that first summer back, it was initially the smells of camp that elicited buried childhood memories. It was the smell of pine, sticky sap, and fish in the lake. It was air so fresh and crisp, wind blowing up over the point in front of me. It was the sound of verdant ferns swishing in the breeze still drenched from an evening shower. Had fifteen years truly passed?

Standing beside the car, with my own children running down the path toward the water, I catapulted back to my youth when my Aunt and Uncle owned this camp. How many fond memories I had of spending time there -- learning to swim at the age of eight, walking the grounds alone, spending precious time with my family and relatives, holding my breath under water and opening my eyes, bloodsuckers and salt, Italian sandwiches from Amato's, laughing, oh so much laughing.

Now in my late forties, I occasionally read magazines that ask me what joy is -- do I have any in my life? I experienced true joy every time I stepped down in flip flops onto that soft, slippery blanket of pine needles at camp. True joy is a feeling of elation simultaneously with peace and contentment. It is living in the moment; other thoughts and concerns do not seep into consciousness as they do throughout the busyness of daily life. It is laughing from the depths of your belly not from the shallow surface. It is taking deep breaths, sighing, smiling without realizing you are doing it.

There is an unmistakable energy at the lake that surrounds and envelops you. There is energy everywhere and surrounding everyone, but I find that at the lake, more people feel the same type of energy more palpably. We don't have to think about it or seek it. It's a calming energy. I've seen even the most uptight people change at the lake; even the lines on their faces soften. They truly relax. Their insides slow down. Like me, the peace of that energy may remind them what joy is.

Seventeen years ago, when our oldest son was two, we wanted a "kid-friendly" vacation. We hired a realtor and drove all around the remote lakes of Maine, with a screaming, car-sick child in the backseat, looking at properties. We only asked for a safe place for Matt to swim and play with his sand toys. We wanted clean, clear water, a bit of a sandy beach with a gradual walk-in for him, and some privacy for us. We wanted to see and hear nature, not other people. We never found what we were looking for. Discouraged, we gave up.

Four years later, when our second son was almost two, we started discussing "kid-friendly" vacations again. (There must be something about two-year-olds and the need to get away!) That winter, for fun, we drove to my Aunt and Uncle's old camp on a lake just forty-five minutes north of our home which they sold when I was twenty.

The one-mile camp road was steep. In summer, as we drove down the curvy, tree-lined hill, I always sang "lions and tigers and bears, oh my!" I think my mother started that tradition. As a child, I thought I might see a rusted Tin Man chopping wood in the thick trees to my right or left -- that's how like the yellow brick road, at the spot of the dark, creepy forest, it looked to me. When I peered into the trees as a child, I expected to see the silver glint of the Tin Man's suit, ax rusted mid-chop above his head.

I never did find that Tin Man, but I always looked every time I passed that section of the camp road. Once running, I saw two deer watching me from the woods, perfectly still....where the Tin Man might have once been.

CHAPTER 2

Dirt Road vs. Durt Road

We drove as far down the snowy road as we could that winter and then trekked in from there. I pulled 5-year old Matt on a plastic sled and Frank carried Ben, just turned one, on his shoulders. The road in winter was only plowed as far as the pavement went, and as I recall, that winter was a "big snow" winter with at least three feet accumulated by that time. When we climbed the last rise and walked down the private road to the point, both of us stopped at the same time. Although he had come there with me as a teenager, Frank didn't remember it. For me, it looked exactly as it had so many years earlier when I came here as a child myself.

Although I had never been to camp in the snow, it was exactly as I remembered, blanketed in a shroud of white like a dream. It was so quiet and tranquil, the lake frozen over. There was no one around as far as we could see. It was complete silence and solitude, broken only by an occasional icicle dropping from a tree branch. Frank stood in front of me looking down the cliff at the expanse of the icy, snow covered lake. Ben suddenly clapped his tiny mittened hands without reason….except pleasure at where he was, where we all were.

"Why didn't you think of this before?" Frank asked me.

"I don't know. I'll call as soon as we get home," I smiled.

Sarah, the owner at that time, lived out of state. The property was about an acre on a point, at the end of Dirt Road (not to be confused with Durt Road which was off the main route) with two camps built by my Uncles with only a nail and string as their architectural guide to keeping walls straight. My Aunt and Uncle were still in contact with her and gave me her telephone number. I called to see if perhaps she rented.

What a pleasant first call we had; there has been karma between us since our first conversation on that call. As family to the original owners, I intrigued her. She did rent one of the camps, my Uncle Harold's, the earlier-built camp. She had fixed up Uncle Jack's for herself.

Uncle Jack's was less rustic with a prettier view of a mountain across the eastern side of the lake, the side where the sun rose. She had done some updating to Uncle Jack's camp by adding a woodstove, pumpkin pine floors, and comfortable furniture. Uncle Harold's was where I had spent my time as a child. It was perfect to me that was the camp she offered to rent us. She said she would be happy to have us come.

It is important I explain that a "camp" to a Mainer can either be a boys or girls recreational camp, or it can be a private family cottage. We use the word interchangeably. A "cottage" to me is a beautiful *Maine Home + Design* magazine type summer home in Southeast Harbor, probably owned by people out-of-state who visit for a few weeks annually. A cottage to me is usually large, although the term itself means a "small home" or "vacation home." For people who own cottages, they probably are smaller than their main home. A cottage to me is more formal or fancy than a camp.

A camp is a rustic place, a get-away. I have relatives who call their winter chalet at Sugarloaf Mountain a camp. If someone talks to you about camps on the lake, they are probably Mainers, and what they may be describing are private family get-away homes. When we talk about recreational camps for children, we probably call them "summer camps." So, this "camp" I write about was a private spot for our family. Our "camp" may be what you call a "cottage."

We rented the camp for nine years, Ben aged one through ten and Matt aged five through fourteen, until Sarah put it up for sale. We've since rented other camps to keep the get-away tradition alive, but none compare to my Aunt and Uncle's due to the experiences and the timing of when we rented, when our children were young.

How we would have loved to buy the camp ourselves, but at $600,000 in 2005, we couldn't financially, even in our dreams. The camp has been lost to me twice in my life now, once at twenty and once at forty-three. That is the reason I write. We should savor things that matter most to us…and never forget. That camp changed my husband and me, and it contributed to the wonderful young men my boys have become who so appreciate nature, peace and quiet.

After our first couple of summers, Sarah stopped renting to anyone except us, but she allowed us to come sometimes off-season and then always spend our vacation mid-summer when her own family were not coming from out West. Going to that camp each summer for nine years became, for my family and me, an authentic slice of heaven. We did not need to own it; we just needed a place to get away, to connect with nature, and to slow down. The familiarity of going to the same place is what created lasting memories and feelings.

CHAPTER 3

Camp Goon

Camp Goon" was christened by Matt that first summer when he was five. I have seen two loons on the lake; they always stay in pairs and together raise their young. Neighbors said there were four who made Crescent Lake their home, but I have only seen two at any given time.

We would say to Matt, "Listen. Listen to the sound of the loons. It's like they're laughing." Their call, or yodel, was eerie, especially deep in the night when we were awakened to them through open camp windows, communicating from one end of the lake to the other.

They are an uncommon looking breed -- jet black with white markings, majestic in their form with their heads sitting close atop their bodies and their pointed black beaks. They are shaped similarly to ducks and are great swimmers. Their eyes are red. The contrast of the ebony and red was alarming, especially when one came up out of the water (they could stay under for a great distance) very near to our canoe, and we were able to get a close look at their uniqueness.

"Mom, listen," Matt would respond back to me. "Listen to the 'goons!'" Hence, the christening of "Camp Goon!"

That summer Matt had Native American toys: a headdress, a tomahawk with feathers. Frank set up our green, nylon four-man tent down on the point and Matt would play in it, wearing the headdress, pretending he was an Indian from the old West.

He dragged a short log from the firewood pile to the front of the tent and used it as his seat. "City boy" drew a fire on a piece of paper to put in front of his log. He would balance on the log, holding a bare stick over his fire, still wearing his headdress, sometimes sporting face paint he insisted I apply. I wondered what he saw on the end of his stick, held carefully over his paper fire. Pretend marshmallow? Weiner?

He would then march up the hill from the point to the camp, thrusting his tomahawk up and down as he did so, making rhythmic calls, self-absorbed in his role-playing.

By the age of fourteen, beginning high school that fall, Matt no longer role-played (in public) but sat on the canvas beach chairs we always put at the point, replacing the tent in those later years. I sat in that spot myself early in the mornings when the sun had just risen across the water or late in the afternoon when I was having my glass of Chardonnay, a few crackers with a Gruyere spread, perhaps some green grapes.

Bushes had grown up in front of the spot where we sat enough to hide us sitting there but not so much that we did not have a perfect view of the lake and the rising sun. Canoes paddled just in front of me while I was sitting in that spot totally unaware of my presence. It was a secret spot, a private spot, a personal spot shared by my son and me.

Often, from the camp or from the dock, I watched Matt when he was sitting there at the point, looking at the lake, alone, absorbed in his thoughts. Sometimes he was tossing stones into the water or skimming them, sometimes playing his acoustic guitar, maybe watching the afternoon sun begin to drop in the sky and cast shadows.

At other times, our high school boy kayaked by himself in the cove, then with the look and build of a man: slim, muscular, angular jaw line. Often, he left his life vest unbuttoned in this safe spot on the lake.

But I could remember the earlier years when he first learned to kayak at nine or ten when he looked so much like L.L. Bear of L.L. Bean storybook fame, his chestnut buzz cut short around his round face, quietly taking in the mountains, the birches and pines that lined the lake, feeling on his legs the dribble of lake water dripping from his paddle as he coasted without paddling, sometimes talking to himself unconsciously.

His red kayak and bright yellow paddle shone against the glistening blue water of early morning or late afternoon. Sometimes, faintly, I would hear him humming or singing low, even as a teenager, as he moved through the water.

Other times at fourteen, he was becoming caught up in the doing and the accomplishing. Some of his rides were not leisurely as they once were. I could tell he was competing against himself to go at a certain chosen speed across the lake, or maintain a complete smoothness as he glided swiftly through the water, or pushed his limits as he actually tried to jump in his craft head on into waves made by speedboats — a sport, a game, a more thrilling ride.

Camp gave our boys and us a means to disconnect and yet connect so much more deeply to each other as a family and to ourselves, our souls. The time we spent at camp changed from year to year in how we approached it, what we did, the relevance of what that time away became to each of our very existences.

There have been times in my life when I've been on stimulation-overload, with people, demands, cars, noise, chaos, and what I call "eye-pollution" -- all the businesses, buildings and signs on the streets where I drove, and I yearned for everything to just stop, just for a minute so I could breathe, so I could collect myself and breathe. Camp was that breath. When there, we decompressed. There was no clock, only the natural bodily rhythms. We looked inward and found strengths and a sense of calm that we called upon when we went back to our real world.

When Matt approached his pre-teen years, we began having chats about girls, respect, peer pressure, and were able to initiate these tough conversations quite comfortably at camp while sitting alone around a campfire or floating on the lake for hours. With no agenda and no schedule, the conversation — his conversation sometimes — brought up subjects we just did not seem to touch during the busyness of our work days and life at home. What was a difficult conversation to begin seemed to flow quite naturally within the relaxed pace of camp.

I bought a book at one year's school Book Fair titled How to Help Your Child Succeed. In it were parenting tips and a short quiz to do with my child. At camp, I did the quiz with Matt and the information about him I learned, quite casually, was amazing! Children who "succeed," according to this book, included those who had a positive relationship with at least one adult other than their parents — Aunts, Uncles, teachers, coaches, neighbors. It asked if the child felt there was an adult with whom he could talk, ask for advice or questions, seek out if he needed help.

Matt named Martha and Ed Crockett who lived up the street from us and Sue Doyon who lived down the street, parents of his two best friends, Mattie Crockett and Syd Doyon. He spent a lot of time in their homes. I had no idea Matt felt he had such a solid relationship with these neighbors and was so pleased he felt this way. I was sure to tell these neighbors when we returned home. What an honor to have an adolescent boy name you as a "friend."

The conversations at camp, mostly because we had the time, no distractions, and were more at peace at our cores, took us in new directions and I learned so much from my boys and from my husband; things I had no idea they might think or care about. In this unhurried and peaceful place, Frank remembered dreams he had years earlier, things he would like to do in his life, places he would still like to see. Somehow, in that beautiful spot, those dreams seemed possible and so they peeked out from the place deep in his mind where he had buried them in the last twenty years, so caught up in realism, making a living, and raising sons.

Camp reminded us that so much was possible and being true to ourselves was important. Our essential selves woke up at camp and began to show who we truly were deep inside. Sometimes, as adults, it was not the person the rest of the world saw on a daily basis.

Because the topics of children can be so random, at camp sometimes the boys would tell stories of three or four years earlier or something that happened on the playground at school in first grade that obviously impacted them but they had never shared with us. Stories or events seemed to spill out at camp because everything had been put on pause, and they remembered.

Look at all we might have missed if we never slowed down to just be with one another.

CHAPTER 4

Downpour

Matt was always a chatter. With me as his Mom and his extroverted Grandmother as his daytime sitter when Frank and I worked, he really had no option! Talking, a lot, was what he knew. We joke that Matt was born talking. Once, at no more than two, he "wowed" his Grandmother's neighbor when he corrected her that the hard wood in the flooring was "actually a rectangle" not a "square" as she was trying to teach him.

When he entered middle school, everything changed. Matt stopped talking. Many responses became one word, and he didn't have an interest in chatting as he once had. He would have talking spurts, on his terms, when he felt like it. I realized the changing dynamic quickly and gave him the space he needed, but made myself available for whenever those spurts happened.

It was a few years earlier that I had coined the term "Family Sundays." It was the one day we did something all together as a family. No friends joined us and no friends came to our house on this one day. Every other day, the boys' friends visited our home. Most of the time, it was all about the boys – their activities, their social events, their sports. But just this one day out of seven….

Our Sundays would be as simple as playing a board game or watching a video or might turn into an overnight in New Hampshire with a long hike in the White Mountains and picnic or a day skiing or a day at the beach. We did whatever we felt like and we rotated who picked the activity.

I found so much merit in "Family Sundays" that I wish I began it earlier in my marriage. It was great for Frank and my sanity. As introverts, one day without several boys running through the house, getting snacks for several, the noise, the chaos was so needed. The time together helped keep the brothers bonded. They are able to spend time with each other, even though they are four years apart, because they always have. They routinely spent time with each other so it became natural and comfortable.

And, I learned that when we were riding up a long chair lift in the cold or hiking three to four hours, Matt would talk. With so much time on our hands and no agenda, he opened up. It was still on his terms and the topics were what he wanted to talk about (mostly music at that point and bands I didn't know like the Shins and Death Cab for Cutie), but I discovered that by having the set Sunday time available kept him connected with us through middle and high school. It also fostered the man he's become and the relationship Frank and I have with him. From college, he talks to us now more, and more deeply, than he ever has before; the talking became a natural part of our relationship.

When he hit his later teen years, with a car, a girlfriend, and a job, Matt spent less time with us. Family Sunday's were no longer weekly. We kept the concept and still did it on occasion, enough to keep us together, but also enough to keep it something he was interested in doing with us. Our vacations at all other times of the year were shortened to weekends as the boys got older instead of weeks. We were trying to meet everyone's needs so we always enjoyed the time we spent together.

Family Sunday's became my little secret for staying connected with my teenage son. It worked beautifully at a critical phase in his life, and I'm charting the same course with son #2.

By the age of fourteen, the dynamic at camp had changed for Matt. I watched and pondered it. He spent more time alone at camp than he ever had before – just playing his guitar or typing on his computer. As creative people, my son and I carry our laptops everywhere. To us, it is not a distraction from nature; it enhances it during extended stays as we write stories or songs or thoughts to capture the moments. So I had no qualms about him bringing his laptop, but was taken aback by how much time he chose to be alone. He didn't get into the lake to swim until Friday of that week.

When we kayaked, if Frank and I headed ours to the right of an island, Matt said, "I'll go this way and meet you around the other side." He would then take off around the left side.

He was not angry or upset. When asked, he told us, of course, he still liked coming to camp. He said, "No issues." I think he meant it. It was not a slight toward us; it was a natural teenage tendency to want to be alone and independent of us.

On about our fifth day that summer, when we took the day's kayak ride, Matt was "on." It was one of the occasions when he wanted to talk. He hung back and kayaked beside me, the slowest one of the group. He questioned me about our family tree, about books I was reading, about World War II which he had studied at school. He rambled.

So caught up in conversation, I didn't notice the black clouds sweeping in quickly from over the mountains. We were quite a long way from our camp. Frank, steering his two-seater "minivan" kayak, knew rain was coming and fast. "We need to head back," he shouted toward us and then took off. When he was little, Ben used to be afraid of thunder and Frank wanted to get him, his kayak-mate in the double "minivan," to shore before it arrived.

Matt leisurely turned his craft homeward, still talking rapidly. He was telling me one of his friends had commented that he had changed; he said Matt had seemed to grow up ahead of the other guys. Matt was testing me for my reaction.

The black clouds were directly overhead by then and I could hear the thunder rumbling over the mountains. I paddled faster, responding to Matt, not wanting to lose this talking streak he was on. Rain began to pour and within five minutes, it was torrential. I could barely see in front of me. Still Matt talked!

Lightening cracked ahead. It bolted all the way down to the lake, jagged and so bright from that close distance. "Matt, paddle, buddy. We're going to have to finish this conversation later. We've gotta go!" I shouted through the driving rain.

Matt looked up, seeing the rain for the first time, and within only a minute, he paddled strongly, as he was now able to do, and left me far behind.

I was scared but was laughing to myself. When he wanted to talk, not even thunder and lightening could stop him. That chatter was still in there; he just didn't visit as often as he used to.

Unfortunately, we never did finish that conversation back in the camp although I tried as I hung our suits near the fire to dry and pulled the rocking chair close to Matt on the couch. He was done. I had my chance and now it was over. I shivered thinking how close that lightening came to me, a lightening rod paddling across the middle of the lake. What I would do to listen to whatever my son had to say.

CHAPTER 5

How the Children Adapted

Ben was eighteen months the first summer we came to camp as a family. The summer he turned seven was an eventful one for Ben, marked by a huge change in his development. Going from age six to seven was a significant milestone. He grew up so much that year and began to show his wonderful sense of humor, very funny faces, and happy-go-lucky personality.

He took swimming lessons in a local pool that spring; at seven that is very late for today's children but Ben was a shy, sensitive kind of guy and would not leave Mom's side at age two or three the first time we enrolled him. Ben was physically more aggressive than Matt so we thought we could teach him to swim ourselves. Imagine parents teaching their children to swim when the time is right for each child. Now it is lessons and children's camps all the way, and they begin as babies. We thought we would try the old-fashioned way of doing it ourselves for free.

At the end of his sixth summer, he was right there, so close to swimming but not quite. After a week in Florida that winter, again, he was right there, so close but not quite. We gave up and enlisted help, but there was no more fearing to leave Mom at the next spring's lessons. By then, he was ready. And finally, he learned to swim! He jumped off the diving board in the deep end at the local pool's lessons, over his head, one of only two children to attempt it. And at camp, he was a different person than the prior summer.

He, too, could venture beyond the end of the dock. He could swim! He was so proud of himself. He could use the noodle or float on a blow-up pillow and come out deep with us. Sometimes, especially when my Mom and sisters, Elisa and Bonnie, visited, we'd hang out half way out in the middle of the lake, just floating in our tubes and chatting.

We floated over the waves in black rubber tire tubes, our legs linked in another's tube until we became an entire network of tubes gliding up and down in unison over the waves. Ben slipped out of his tube purposely, wearing his mask, to view all of us from below the water's surface. He kept bobbing back up into the hole of his tube and slipping back down without a sound.

Ben even tried the snorkel. He was a thin child and got cold easily. In prior years, he would get into the water reluctantly and then only stay in a few minutes, shivering in the still-cold July lake water. Beginning in his seventh year, he was the first one in and the last one out. He swam at night. He absolutely reveled in this newfound joy.

And to think, our first summer when he was only eighteen months, he would not stay still to do anything more than two to three minutes…. and neither could I. I chased him all over the camp grounds. He tripped over tree roots; he ate the pine needles; he got splinters in his feet from the wooden dock; he splashed himself in the face by accident, crying and crying, water up his nose. He would stand naked in three inches of lake water, after we removed his bloated diaper, playing with his purple submarine and scuba men and sing "Take me out….BAWL game….take me out….CWOUD. Buy me PEANUTS and CWACK JACKS!!"

He trembled all over with excitement when he saw the ducks swim by so close to the shore. He said repeatedly, "Mama-duck, Mama-duck" as she floated by at the head of a swimming line of baby ducks.

His first summer, we also learned something about Ben we might never have learned if not at camp. When riding in our small, aluminum boat around the lake each evening, at odd times, Ben would become extremely upset and try to get up off his metal seat and climb out of the boat. We could not understand what was coming over him. He was just suddenly, and randomly it appeared, agitated and upset by something.

It was not until the next year that we learned what it was, when he could verbalize his fear to us. He was afraid of A-frame camps. A-frames are small camps or ski chalets that are shaped like a triangle, like an "A." There were only a couple on our lake but sure enough, each time we would ride by one, he could not look at it. When we tried to learn what it was about A-frames that frightened him, he could not explain. To this day, he cannot explain. It is kind of an odd fear. And where did it come from?

When I was relating this to someone recently, they asked if Ben was intuitive, psychic maybe. He is not that I am aware of although the one time I met with a psychic, it was Ben and Ben's "light" she dwelled on while saying nothing of Matt. Someone suggested it was something about A-frames that triggered a past life. I will not go there....to me, it was just a highly unusual fear for which we have no explanation and about which we may never have known had we not gone to the lake and passed an A-frame camp.

Away AT A CAMP IN MAINE

My video of that first summer shows an adorable baby walking around the grounds just as the sun is sneaking up over the tree line wearing his PJ's, moccasin slippers, and a red polar fleece jacket with planets and crescent moons, babbling inaudibly, and clapping those hands again on occasion in moments of unrestrained joy. He kept walking up close to the lens, putting his face on the glass to see himself in the reflection, those chubby cheeks so soft looking even on film, drool dripping from the corner of his pink lips. That video captured the boy who is now in high school – over six feet tall, thin, and a swimmer.

That first summer, I bathed him in one of the tiny double camp sinks. That's how tiny my little, blond, beautiful boy was. The sink was so small, it just fit our plates; it would not fit a slightly larger platter. Now our "baby" is fifteen and he is a funny man so sure of himself and so happy in the company of his older brother and his look-alike Dad, coming into his own.

CHAPTER 6

Holding Hands

fter years of renting, we had a simple rhythm to moving in. It was a lot of work to get there and then get us back home, but each precious minute in between was worth every bit of effort. Becoming more clever over the years, we created an Excel spreadsheet that we referenced each year of what to bring and checked things off as we piled them up to load in the cars. The piling up generally began a week in advance.

When Sarah offered to let us come and go off-season because of our proximity to the camp, we laughed. "Sarah, you come with an overnight bag at most. We come with two cars and a truck!"

With children, we did not travel lightly and our getting away did not happen on the spur of the moment or by happenstance. Baby play pens, large yellow trucks for the sand, picture books, and lots of toys to bring turned into Harry Potter chapter books and Gameboys, and then laptops, iPods, and guitars to lug. Although some of their "stuff" became smaller and later they could carry it themselves, it did not seem like our load lessened.

Maybe someday it would and my mother reminded me regularly that whether I knew it or not, whether or not I felt stress, those would be the happiest times of my life and I should not wish them away. I should savor that "work" and being needed because it would not last forever and like so many parents do, I would mourn the loss and replay those happy times together all the rest of my days.

Life is not about work and how much of it we do. It will be the time spent with our children at camp, the passing of their youth, marked by the changes we saw in what they were able to do there, outdoors, with no schedules, no limitations, no peer pressure. It was their reactions to new sights and experiences. It was the conversations with them we remember, sitting around campfires late at night, when we took the time to just be with them, no agenda.

I remember a campfire night with friends visiting when we were playing an alphabet word game. Each person around the circle had to think of a word using the next letter of the alphabet and give the others clues to guess that word. At eight or nine, Matt's letter was "Z." The clue he offered was "It's the little pill you take when you're not feeling quite like yourself."

The word he had come up with for "Z" was not "zoo" or "zebra" or "zipper," words we might have expected a child his age to know. His word was Zoloft. I was astounded. Where had he heard Zoloft? I learned he had heard it on a T.V. commercial and his clue was actually the jingle. I laughed thinking my friends, no doubt, thought it was something he had read in my medicine cabinet.

It is the sound of their laughter in our videos taken, and their relaxed smiles in photographs that are deeply entrenched in our memory banks. We have photos of the boys and their friends, dripping wet as they've just come out of the lake, their arms carelessly thrown over each others' shoulders, long wet bangs flipped to the sides, smiling, laughing, so happy to be right there, right then, together. Their faces in those pictures show pure joy.

We have videos of "kayak wars" when groups of the boys would play bumper cars in kayaks and joust with their paddles.

We have some "series" photos, like still frames, taken of Ben and a friend, preparing to jump off the end of the dock — there they were running down the plank; there they were midair above the water, noses plugged and eyes squeezed shut; there was the splash of water when they plunged deeply within it; and there were their wet heads as they popped up, laughing hysterically.

We have photos of relatives visiting who have now passed away. They were wearing long cotton pants, sun hats, big sunglasses and sitting at the lakeshore in those old fashioned metal chairs with the brightly colored plastic weave on the seat and back that folded up flat and were easily carried to picnics on the water. Those chairs were better for older people because they were higher, like regular kitchen chairs, not sand chairs that they had to fall into and roll out of in order to stand up.

In one photo, Ben was no more than two sitting in a child-size Adirondack chair, eating Cheerios out of a plastic bowl, wearing a white, hooded terry cover up and purple "jelly" sandals that Frank was mortified when I bought. For God's sake, those were girls' shoes! Ben was two and they were soft and made of rubber, perfect in my mind for slipping on at the lake pre-Croc days. And purple was the only color they had....probably because they were girls' shoes.

Those videos and photos tell the story of our passing years at camp. We all changed so much in how we looked from year to year — which hair styles were in, weight up, weight down, aging. Babies becoming children, becoming teenagers, becoming men. The effort of arranging that time away, planning it, and getting us there proved very worthwhile.

Each year the coming and going for Frank and me seemed to get easier. Frank and I knew our individual "jobs." We knew where we liked to put the food (on the counter of a small cupboard - not enough room inside); who slept in which bed (Ben in the back bedroom with the blue curtain for its door, Matt in the double-sized mattress on noisy springs in the tiny loft, Frank and me in the small middle bedroom with the red curtain as its door and the antique coat rack on which to hang our clothes).

Extra toilet paper went by the kitchen stove outside the bathroom and our toiletries stayed in our duffel under the bathroom sink - the tiniest medicine cabinet we had ever seen, just big enough to hold our toothbrushes and sunscreen and glance in the mirror to run a comb through wet, never blow-dried, hair.

Supermarket produce bags lined trash cans and bread bags replaced ziplocs. No Williams Sonoma kitchenware, only Wal-Mart Teflon purchased over forty years before and mismatched yard sale dishes and cups. The oven ran hot and the fridge ran cold. We brushed the occasional ants from the counter and stepped on them – pest control. No biggie. Nothing was a biggie.

We learned what worked best; all was within reach, nothing fancy but practical and easy. Our settling in became smooth and orderly with our years of practice. The less time we spent setting up, the more time we could spend sitting down.

At camp, there was no rushing. There was a lot of sitting, together and alone, observing, listening, being. We all did a lot of nothing and when we felt like doing a little something, we waded, swam, read, walked the narrow dirt roads, played Scrabble. Ben won his first game against us at age six. Never would we have believed, having just ended first grade, he could even play Scrabble without a partner, but only the slowdown of the camp pace without video or computer games allowed him the opportunity to try.

Why is it that at home in suburbia, we toiled weekly for perfectly manicured lawns complete with paying lawn care services to spray chemicals on them? We rushed to our full-time jobs which were certainly cutting short our life spans, to soccer games, PTA meetings, and church when we could drag ourselves out of bed on Sunday mornings, the one day of the week that even God rested.

Being at camp allowed Frank and me to catch up, to talk not just about "who's on first" but about what was still important to us, what our dreams were, what we would like to do. In our early married years of new jobs and new babies, I can remember times when we did not talk about anything other than our schedule — "who's on first" — for a matter of days due to exhaustion and focusing solely on the children's needs.

It was discouraging to me at times to think that is what we had become and frightening to think it might be the way it would be from there on out. Frank was my best friend and had been since we were thirteen. You've heard the term soul mate? Our relationship has weathered many changes in us and the world around us and yet we hang in there. We have grown apart for periods of time as we mature and change out of life's necessities but always come back to each other.

At camp, we sat in the Adirondack chairs on the shore of the lake, late in the evening when the boys were sound asleep and talked about whatever was important to us... like we used to when we were younger, freer. We didn't talk about schedules, finances, jobs, what we needed to do, or everything that was wrong in the world. We sat and watched shooting stars in the black night sky and talked or didn't talk. We could just be together and enjoy the peaceful company of the best friend we each had for more than half our lifetimes. Quietly, we held hands.

Chapter 7

Rec-reate

I told Frank that I enjoyed watching him at camp as much as I enjoyed watching the lake. He was another person at camp, completely different from whom he was day-to-day, and it became more pronounced with each passing year. I imagined seeing the stress seep out of his ears, slowly at first in small wisps when we arrived and were caught up with settling in, and then like a rush of air as he deflated the persona he pulled on to wear to work each day until all that was left was the core. All that was left was the true Frank.

The only responsibilities he had were pulling the kayaks onto the beach at dusk, pulling the sand chairs up off the dock so they did not blow away, teaching his boys to fish and enjoy what he considered the finer things in life.

As I chatted, read, and helped the boys settle into bed at night, Frank always went down to the lake in the pitch dark. Early morning is my favorite time of day and I have learned that if I spend some alone time then, a positive and energetic tone has been set for me for the entire day, and I am so much better prepared to face anything that comes my way.

For Frank, it is the night. He worked the early shift so being able to "stay up late" on vacation was part of the treat. He enjoyed spending some time before bed quietly. He would sit alone for a long time just listening. He grew up with the television constantly on. At home, he always has it on, as background noise. At camp, he would not even consider it. Aside from the news, he did not want to see a T.V. or hear a telephone.

We started renting pre-cell phone days, but later when we all owned them, for Frank and me, they were never turned on at camp. If we stayed too connected to home, we were unable to disconnect sufficiently and would lose the benefit of what the get-away was.

Frank fished each day. He kayaked straight across the lake to the narrow, shallow stream that emptied out of the lake into a marshy area all the way to the beaver dam, which was the end of the journey. He tied his large float to the end of the dock and lay in the sun....for hours. On it, he always fell asleep.

There was a period when I was convinced Frank had that deficiency disease where people craving sunlight get physically ill, a vitamin D deficiency or something. We hear of diseases like that living in Maine where we are expected to hold on through our long, cold winters. Frank loves the feel of sunlight on his body; he loves to run when it is ninety-five degrees when lesser runners pass out; he tans even in the winter and for a couple of winters, he would get a cold from late October through the end of May, just kind of a dismal nasty feeling of not being up to par. I still believe it was a sunlight deficiency.

Frank attached himself to a word at camp. One day, while lying on his float, he lifted his head off the air-pillow and said, "rec-reate." Not "re-create" as the dictionary lists — to begin anew — but "rec-reate" making a verb out of "recreation."

"What?" I asked, not understanding.

He repeated, "Rec-reate. That's what I was made to do. Rec-reate. I was made to rec-reate." A big smile from ear to ear and his head dropped back down onto the air pillow.

Yes, he was.

Frank is the hardest worker I know, always busy, always moving, but he did love to go to camp and do nothing.

It's the only place where he did so. There is a difference between living and living well and it has nothing to do with money or useless busyness. A good life is all about balance. A good life is about feeling joy, true joy. It is about contentment.

My Maid of Honor from our wedding, Sally, came to stay with us at camp one summer. She lived in California for several years. I did not realize how right my invitation was, and it is because of her that I wrote this little book. Within the first thirty minutes she was with us at camp, with the warm late afternoon wind blowing up the hill off the lake, caressing her cheeks and tousling her hair, she took a deep breath of the lake air and said, "Everyone needs this. Everyone needs this whether they know it or not."

I think she is right. Before I just thought it was right for us and for our family, but I saw from her that it is right for all human beings, all families.

I have read and loved dearly travel books like <u>Bella Tuscany</u> or <u>A Year in Provence</u> written by retired couples moving to Europe and fixing up villas or old farmhouses. I want to share the equally wonderful experiences of getting away, even to a place as close as a forty-five-minute drive from your home, when you are younger and what those times mean in the growth and development of your children. The memories and feelings will last their lifetimes and the rest of yours.

There is no need to wait until retirement, until you have stopped or slowed down. In fact, the joy and peace you will experience will expand exponentially in your life as a younger working person so that even your "real" life will benefit and grow in a more positive way due to these getaways and reconnections with your authentic self. What these times will show you is what is truly important to you. You will release stress, concern, tension. What you will receive is clarity.

A friend said to me once that she would hate such a private get away with her husband. "He'd go crazy," she said.

"You think so?" I probed. "You might be surprised."

"And he'd try to corner me when he had me and talk about everything that makes me mad."

"Really? What makes you mad?"

"You know, finances and stuff."

"Oh, no. That's not what going away to camp is at all! Frank and I don't talk about anything like that. We don't talk about the same things we talk about at home. Because we don't need to. That week or two or entire summer away is so removed from your neighborhood and your house and day-to-day lives, if you let it be, that you truly shouldn't talk about those everyday things, or you've missed your opportunity for rejuvenation. You've missed the point."

She just stared at me.

"Frank and I talk about our old dreams and what happened to them. We dream new dreams. We talk about trips we want to go on or plans for our future."

"Really? You do?" my friend said, and then I saw it was starting to sink in. I'm not sure if she believed she and her husband could do this, but at least she heard me and she was processing the idea.

At the lake, I liked to read nonfiction about Maine, like the history of Mount Desert or places Down East, Northeast or Southeast Harbor. Although from Maine, I grew up and spent most all of my time in southern Maine, Portland. Rarely, did my parents take us kids north. Frank and I first visited Bar Harbor and Acadia National Park, just four hours north of Portland, in our thirties and Frank kept saying the whole time we were there — "Why have we not been here before?" We loved it. We loved the park with its miles of hiking trails, its stone bridges and carriage trails, its rocky coastline, and so many green trees.

We didn't visit Rangeley, Maine until our mid-forties and again marveled at our not coming sooner. We fell in love with Rangeley and its expansive views of mountains and lakes. The town itself is right out of a Stephen King novel, a throw back to the 1950's where all the locals know each other, and out-of-towners stick out like a sore thumb. We love it in the winter when the temperature falls below zero, and we must run from our room in the only inn in town to the dining room or to our skis mounted on the post outside the lodge. We love it in the summer when everything is so green, and there are just trees, trees, trees.

I never tire of looking at green trees and Maine is abundant with them. If you travel far north and drive the turnpike, you might get very bored of green trees. That's all there is – green trees, millions and millions of them. But, I never tire of looking at them, breathing in their scent, especially the pines.

When I kayaked the lake, sometimes I smiled because the smell was exactly the smell of those small pine pouches they sell in gift shops all over Maine. Those little pouches, although a little overwhelming in scent when you first purchase them, are truly what the pine trees in Maine smell like and on the lake, where there are hundreds of them, they smell exactly like those pouches.

When I'm in the nature of Maine, surrounded by the trees and underbrush, the huge gray rocks on the shoreline and in the lake, with mountains surrounding me, under a gorgeous blue sky with white puffy clouds, I am proud to be a Mainer and so happy to be alive. I slow way down. I am far outside my day-to-day life so want to learn and read something different than I read in my bed at home before going to sleep.

Day reading at the lake, sitting in the sun on a dock or curled up in front of a fire, was a different experience so I wished to read something different, no motivational or self-help books up there. I wanted to know more about

this beautiful state that surrounded me and dream about
new places in it to visit. I envisioned my next adventure —
where and when it would be.

Reading at the lake made me dreamy. I read in the heat
of the sun feeling spacey and far away. I became absorbed
in the characters and the places, their lakes or oceans, their
camps, their daily happenings. And I understood them.
My family would bring me back from time to time and
I paused to swim, or watched canon ball jumps from the
dock or attempts at dives, or I went boating or tubing with
them. But then I slipped back into that other world that
was my reading life, enveloped in that imagery and those
characters who sometimes felt as real to me as my own
family.

Sometimes, as we all sat reading, all lost in our own
worlds, we commented to those around us about what we
just read. Sometimes it began an in depth conversation.
At other times, we all just stayed quiet, semi-snoozing, not
wanting to break that calmness of feeling so relaxed in the
sun, not wanting to stir anything up.

At camp, it was so important to get lost inside ourselves,
inside nature, inside water and sunshine and storms.
Spending time with friends and relatives had its place, but
being alone was what fueled us. It is what brought out our
creative sides whether we knew we had such sides or not.
If we stopped, looked and felt gratitude, we began to have

thoughts and ideas that compelled us to write, paint, sing, dance, draw, take photographs.

Human beings are complex animals. We can work fifty years using our left brain, numbers crunching or serving clients in some capacity, but we still have a right brain. To earn a living, left brained people seem to find more work and make more money. We haven't yet as a culture come to grips with our right sides and the value they bring to us as a society. If more people get away, such as this, and discover their right brains, it's possible society's perceptions will change over time.

Certainly, we do recognize and elevate some who use their right sides of their brains - authors, artists, actors, singers - but it is my belief that everyone is born with a creative side and if encouraged and cultivated to bring it out, something that getting away in nature promotes and stimulates, all of us may become more proficient in bringing it out in our everyday lives. We would find more peace and balance in becoming the totality of what we're meant to be.

CHAPTER 8

My Own Memories

My memories of camp when I was a child, when my Aunt and Uncle owned it, are many. They are memories that leave me with a warm sensation deep in my gut, deep in my soul, I think. I always looked forward to coming. My folks would arrive around noon for the day and stay until well after dark, after my bedtime. Often, they would let me get into my pajamas before leaving, after I had taken one more swim in the lake and washed my body and hair with Ivory soap. My long, dark hair was combed neatly and dripped down the back of my nightdress.

After that last swim, padding back up the hill to the camp in my flip flops, tip-toeing, trying not to get my clean feet dirty, I would slip into my PJ's in one of the bedrooms while my parents and Aunts and Uncles laughed and talked, right up until the moment we left. I felt soft and warm, clean and content. I would be asleep before our car turned off the camp road, dreaming of my day in the sun.

When I was eight, my parents were trying to teach me to swim but I just was not catching on, ironically just like my son, Ben. My difficulty was that I would not get my face wet and without getting your face wet, swimming is nearly impossible. Neighbors from home were coming to visit us at camp, with my buddies. They all swam, my folks told me. Wouldn't I like to be able to swim with them? They tried, again, to teach me to swim that morning before our guests arrived.

My mom held my belly, laying me out flat across the water, hoping her gentle support would be enough to show me how to float and get me moving my arms and legs.

No go. Each time she slid her hand out from under my belly, I would immediately drop my legs and stand up. I wanted no part of it.

Just before lunchtime, our friends showed up. Their children were so happy to be at the lake, something I could tell they did not do often. They ran straight down to the water and jumped in. They swam out deep, back and forth. They dove. They bobbed up and down, in and out of the water, fifty, one hundred times without stopping. I sat on the dock, smiling, vicariously enjoying their play. Without a word, all at once, I got off the dock and swam. That was it. There was no more discussion, no more help. And I could. My wanting to be included and play with my pals got me to swim without any more protests. I just did it.

I so enjoyed hanging out with my older cousins at camp — Corliss, Tommy, Cindy. I was "the kid," ears and eyes wide open listening to their stories of junior high and then high school and boys and how to shave your legs the correct way, being sure to get that spot behind your knee.

In the early 1970's, we would sing at the top of our voices, "Jeremiah was a bullfrog......" and then burst out laughing after a stanza. I did not know the whole song like they did; it was the first line, yelled as loudly as we could in unison, that was the fun. My grandfather's name was Jeremiah. Although we called him Big Bonnie, never Jere or Jeremiah, our knowing that name was his gave the song significance to us.

We would lie on the dock, sunning ourselves for hours, and my white Irish skin would usually burn since sunscreen was not part of our going-to-camp items to pack in the early 1970's. I remember my two-piece bathing suits bought at K-Mart, my pudgy, pre-teen belly hanging over my bottoms. Never in my childhood can I recall anyone commenting on my weight, even though years later I found my weight card from the third grade that said at eighty-eight pounds, I was "moderately heavy."

Not kids, not my Dad, and especially not my Mom ever criticized my weight; they didn't seem to even notice. Back then, we were weighed and measured each year in school, not just at the doctor's office. However, puberty, which hit me in the fifth grade, simply took the weight off; it had nothing to do with me or my will power. My baby fat was never a big deal because no one made it a big deal.

Once I tried swimming under a raft like a friend of mine did. I did not like it at all. From that first attempt, I have had a fear of being underwater, confined and unable to breathe. Although I had no trouble or no shortage of air stored to get me to the other side of the raft, the fear of possibly needing to come up before the end of the raft and being trapped was a horrible feeling for me of sheer terror. And to be funny, my friend spun the raft while I was under it. With my eyes open, when I saw that, it was like a topsy turvy dream and I just wanted to get out of there.

The first time I saw the black thing on my shin, I had no idea what it was. I stood in the water, looking down at it and tried to pick it off thinking it was a leaf or piece of grass. My mother was watching me from the shore and knew immediately what it was. It was a bloodsucker, a leech. There is no pulling a bloodsucker off. My Mom, not one for handling panic well, screamed and ran up the path to the camp shouting, "Quick! Get the salt! Kimmy's got a bloodsucker! Oh-h-h-h! Quick!"

My Uncle came into the water and scooped me up off my feet. He carried me to one of the beach chairs and soon my mother was back with the canister of Morton salt. She poured it right onto the black slug and instantly, he curled himself up and dropped off my shin, dead, onto the ground. There was a tiny spot of blood on my leg where he had punctured my skin. I had been sitting on an old log lying in the lake. In a storm, it had fallen from the shoreline and no one ever cut it or hauled it away. It had become slimy after so much time soaking in the water. They determined I must have gotten the bloodsucker near that log.

Every time we visited camp, I would always take a walk around the grounds which satisfied my innate desire to roam, see new things, and be alone. I am an introvert. As a child I did not know there was a word for it; I just did what came naturally for me.

I have always been creative, imaginative, and pensive. I was alone as a child for seven years before my sister, Elisa, arrived and learned how to play alone and entertain myself. I was friendly, but I was most satisfied just being by myself and within my own head.

I created so many adventures and personas for myself on different spots of the camp grounds. I grew to know the land intimately by spending so much time walking around, observing, sitting on the earth, touching the ferns and the trees, gazing at the sparkling sunshine on the lake, becoming hypnotized watching waves lap the shore at the point, lying on my belly observing at close range the "snake spit" on stems of grasses or a monarch butterfly, how feather light and graceful they were.

I observed, and details and colors and sensations seeped deep inside me. I retrieve and replay them at will and they still provide me with great pleasure and peace.

At camp, as a child, I was free. I was happy. I was alive with all my senses experiencing a world so different from my little neighborhood where I was growing up, in the "city," if you will.

I have heard there are several life-changing events in a person's life, turning points, milestones. The time I spent at camp as a child undoubtedly was one of my turning points; it is unquestionably linked to the person I have become. It became so engrained in me that so many years later, it would pull me back. Being outside in nature, seeing new natural settings and appreciating all the wonder around me, is what gives me my greatest joy. I am innately curious and observant. I experience the world in Technicolor with all my senses.

My son has said, to him, it doesn't matter where he is; place doesn't matter. To my Mom, such a strong extrovert, place doesn't matter; it's the company she keeps that matters to her. Conversely, to me, it's all about the place.

My environment is what sets the tone for my body and my mind. Places of beauty, calm, and serenity are where I feel the most comfortable and the most like me. I can be in the natural world with no effort; it is a most natural fit. Whenever in nature, I take deep gulps of the air trying to suck in all of what is "real" around me – nothing tainted or artificial or man made. I am trying to capture it inside of me, thinking that as a human creature, breathing in that fresh air will sustain and nourish me.

While others are looking for the short cuts, I always take the path that is most beautiful to me even if it's a longer journey. I do it when I walk or bike or drive a car. I coined the term "eye pollution" years ago. I cannot drive a Route I, with many stores, signs, cars and chaos. My head gets all crazy and jumbled up. That is what makes me feel stress and unease.

I will always take the back country road even if it's many miles longer. Green is my favorite color and there is nothing more beautiful than lots of green foliage and old trees after copious amounts of rain have fallen. When wet, the green becomes a deep emerald color. It may take me more time going the scenic route, but when I arrive at my destination, I will be me, not Godzilla in a skirt.

CHAPTER 9

The Loft

My Aunt and Uncle's old camp was roughly twenty by twenty-four feet in size, one floor with a tiny loft at the front with a wooden ladder that pulled down. It had running water and electricity but it was rustic. Two brief showers in a row, after washing up the breakfast dishes, was hot water capacity. The third to shower had to wait until the water reheated.

The camp was basically four bare board, uninsulated walls. The walls around the center bedroom were only seven feet high; they did not go to the rafters so we were basically living in one room. When the boys were small, and unaccustomed to living in one room, we all had to go to bed at the same time. We tried everything, turning out lights, whispering, but they could not fall asleep feeling like we were right in the same room with them and probably doing something more fun than sleeping!

Then, in the mornings, they were up at first light and I am talking five a.m. in summer....for the day! There were no curtains and windows were all the way around so the morning light just poured in. By 11:00 a.m., we'd feel like it must be mid-afternoon.

Just like everything, they grew accustomed to the camp set up. Being outside all day in the fresh air exhausted them and they fell asleep within minutes of turning out their small lamps, a benefit to taking small children away. I always wonder about people with sleep problems. I have found that lots of fresh air, exercise, and a peaceful core seem to bode well for regular sleep patterns. At ten or eleven, Matt was known to sleep until 8:30 some days at camp, something he never did at home at that age; he was always up by 6:00 or 7:00 a.m.

One night, Ben suddenly said, "I think I'll take a little nap."

A little nap? I had never heard those words uttered from either of my sons willingly. It was later than I realized; it was bedtime. His body knew it clearly, and he wanted his rest. A friend has said to me of her time at her beach house with her sons, "We eat when we're hungry. We sleep when we're tired. The simple rhythm just falls into place with no effort." So true.

There were no closets in the camp. There were nails pounded right into the wood walls with coat hangers. We hung our minimal clothes, beach towels, baseball caps, straw hats, and life jackets all together on those nails. At camp, I wore the same denim shorts for a week and had no problem slipping on a wool sweater with mud on the elbow and a missing button, which must have popped off from a too-tight life jacket and might have been sitting on the floor of the boat.

At home, the boys might wear two or three outfits in a day including workout clothes while at camp they just pulled the same ones on day after day when they wished to wear something other than a bathing suit. The air or woodstove dried everything to re-use. Even minimizing clothing was freeing.

Much of what was used to build the camp came from the dump or giveaways, all the windows did. They were all different. The bedroom windows had small panes (and cobwebs when the summer season began each year). The windows pulled down to open. To keep them shut there was a nail placed into a hole in the top of the woodwork. We pulled the nail in or out when you opened or shut the window. When the window was open, the nail hung from a string from the top piece of woodwork.

In the front "picture" window there was a bubble in the glass toward the bottom. It was always a talking point when people came to visit us at camp; it looked like a defect in the glass and it was right there smack-dab in the center of such a beautiful view of the lake. It was not a defect. It was from a BB my cousin Tommy shot mistakenly at the camp as a teenager.

I am not sure if that was after he hooked a neighbor in the back with a fishing hook or after he got "duck itch" and had to wear pink lotion all over his chest and back to stop from scratching or after he learned to stay under water for so long it was frightening to anyone watching him swim. Tommy learned to swim like a fish by living at camp for the duration of every summer throughout his childhood.

The décor at camp was eclectic and homey. Sarah had the inside painted white with French blue trim. It made it look more like a cottage than "camp" to me. My rustic camp preference is always the knotty pine interior with green paned windows and a gray stone fireplace.

The first year we came back, my Aunt's furniture was still in the camp which made it even more of a blast from the past, her cups and saucers in the cupboards, her large black glass ball with the net around it hanging in the corner where it had hung for many years. When the pieces were brought to camp they were just furniture….but by the time we returned, so many years later, they had become antiques, the mahogany dining table and buffet, hutch and old bureau. They had a musty smell after years of use.

Sarah replaced the old black cast iron woodstove with a new metal one. The old one's door dropped off each time you opened it and when it was burning hot, it was a tad frightening.

The side door to the camp was on a tight spring. It was an ancient wooden door, painted barn red which, as soon as you let it go, banged against the casing with great force. The sound of that banging door was one I only heard at camp. Bang! Bang! Like the smells of camp, the banging of that door set off a cascade of memories and feelings for me. The door opened onto a wooden deck with beautiful water views from every angle.

We have an alarm system at home (in Maine, one of the safest U.S. states) but at camp, we did not even lock the door. Nothing anyone would want to steal. The need for possessing just was not there.

Camp was not about stuff. It was about the profound beauty of unspoiled nature we still have in abundance in many parts of our nation; the sparkle of sunlight on a windswept lake in summer; the many shades of green leaves on trees; the pale pink of dainty lady slippers which, although becoming extinct, I've seen many in my life; the midnight blue of tiny wild blueberries on the bush; the scream which escaped me each time my body dunked into lake water; and the long sighs which gushed out as I sat looking at a brilliant full moon hanging just over the tree line.

It was about being alone as a family and as a person. It showed me something I tried to carry in my heart all the rest of the year….less is truly so much more.

The kitchen, dining area and living area were one open forum. There were books to share on the bookshelf, Monopoly and Scrabble left by my cousins twenty years ago, and a tattered braided rug in the center of the room. Above the living area was the tiny loft. It fit one double and one single mattress on springs. The boys could almost sit up on the mattresses without hitting their heads on the steep pitch of the roof; adults could not. I am the only adult I know who ever ventured up there.

As a child, rarely was I allowed to go up and it was always such a treat when they finally said I could. It was like a secret spot, a private place to play out my fantasies of adventure. What child would not love that? Between the two mattresses, right along the camp's center line, was a wooden beam to the tip of the roof and behind it, a tiny screened window, no more than eight by twelve inches. The window rolled open and the breeze that blew through seemed greater than a one-foot window would allow. I could hear the wind as it whipped through that small window.

My boys hid popsicle sticks with their names and date at the far ends of the loft, beside the mattresses. They hid painted rocks with their names and date on them. They were usually still there when we returned year-to-year. Occasionally, they were gone which always led to great speculation of who found them and took them and what they thought when they found them and what they might have done with them. It led to leaving some other token in an even tougher hiding spot.

I never denied my boys from going up because of how much I enjoyed it as a child myself. The ladder stayed permanently down when we rented. When they were young they never dared to sleep up there but as they got older, they would ask me, and I always said yes with a smile but a bit of reluctance. When Ben was younger, if he wished to, I felt I had to stay up there with him so he would remember where he was if he woke in the night and would not walk off the edge. I knew I would bang my head on the roof and have to use the bathroom myself in the night.

And then there was the time I saw a huge cobweb just as I turned to switch off the lamp and put down my book. I climbed down to get a paper towel and wiped it away…. and then dreamed about it. I did not move my body one inch on my mattress the whole night; I was thinking of creeping spiders. And then, perhaps it was real or perhaps I just imagined it, but I REALLY felt something crawling on my bare leg UNDER the covers. If that didn't freak me out when I was dreaming of spiders lying on a musty smelling mattress on a yellowed pillow that was over thirty years old, in the roof of a camp, I don't know what would.

If it began to thunder right then, as it did a few nights later that summer, I would have been all done! And yes, that became an authentic slice of heaven for me as I told you before. When do I get to feel excitement and fright and the novelty of sleeping on a mattress in the rafters, with the glorious moon shining through a one-foot window right beside my head while listening to my first-born peacefully breathing beside me and the call of the loons?

CHAPTER 10

My Uncles

My Uncle Harold was a meticulous man. He was born around 1920, that "greatest" of generations. He had a good mind, a logical, thinking mind. We invited him to visit each time we stayed at camp and he and my Aunt Eileen always came. They were in their seventies that first summer they came back to visit, but I could tell it was bringing them back to times long since forgotten even more than it did me.

They walked all around, very slowly, and looked and looked. They had owned the camp for their three children's entire youth. They moved the family up each year for the entire summer. My Aunt didn't work so was able to stay there with my cousins and run it and their days the way she did at home; my Uncle commuted back and forth to South Portland each day to work.

I know my Uncle enjoyed camp; I could see it in his face and the tender way he raked and tidied up around the property. I'm not sure how much my Aunt enjoyed it. I only ever saw my Aunt cleaning and sweeping and recall her coming down to the lake only on a couple of occasions when I was a kid visiting. I never saw her swim.

Perhaps she did enjoy it when no one was visiting. I can only hope so. Like me, and so many women, in her efforts to do so much, she might have slept through the journey, dreaming only of the finished product and the destination.

I think their generation was more industrious and less seeking of joy than later generations have become. Sometimes ownership brings responsibilities that negate the chance to simply be and simply enjoy because they were too preoccupied with what needed to be done.

To truly vacation, I need to leave my home. Just like my Aunt and Uncle, I find too many things at home needing attention to simply chill and relax and play. I have to be taken out of my environment to stop.

My Uncle was built like Ronald Regan. He was a tall, broad shouldered man and my Aunt, with age and

Parkinson's Disease, was petite. He held her elbow as they walked around the property when they came to visit us. He made a little sucking sound with his mouth and teeth as he stood with his hand cupped over his eyes to block the strong sunlight, despite wearing those plastic sunglasses older people wear that even block sun from coming in the sides of their eyes, to see how the shingles on the roof were holding up.

He told us the story of roofing the camp one summer. It was "hotter than Hades," he said, on that day. Sucking sound, "Did a good job," my Uncle said quietly to only himself.

When they left, he called me as soon as he got home. "Kimmy," he said. "I think there's a problem with the ladder to the loft."

"What?" I said, unsure what he was trying to tell me.

"The piece of wood that holds that ladder up has a short part and a long part." I looked across the room at that piece of wood.

"Yes."

"I think the long part was across the ladder."

"Well, yes. Shouldn't it be? To hold up the ladder?"

"Oh no," he said. "The short part goes across the ladder. The weight of the ladder pushes against it and the long piece acts as the balance to offset its weight. I'm afraid if you have it the wrong way, that ladder's going to fall."

Well, well. I turned the piece of wood the way my Uncle suggested. I would have never realized the point of it. The ladder may have fallen. I bet he thought of that the whole way home.

He and his three siblings purchased the land for the camp more than forty years ago. What they paid a total of $6,000 for was sold thirty years later for over $600,000. It was just over an acre on a point, totally private. Because it was a point, there was a view of the lake three-quarters of the way around, nearly a thousand feet of water frontage. Each of the four siblings intended to build a small camp on the property. Two did and by the time the last two wished to, it was too late. The town had changed property ordinances, especially on waterfront building, and the codes would no longer permit two more camps to be built on the piece of land.

My Uncle Harold was the first to build....but it was not the camp that came first; it was the six by ten foot bunkhouse behind the camp. In the early days, when their three children were small, they would come and sleep in the bunkhouse. My cousin Cindy recalls seven relatives and Tippy the dog sleeping in a line of sleeping bags on the floor of the bunkhouse, with no facilities. I can't imagine it now with the overwhelming smell of boat fuel in the bunkhouse.

My cousins' experiences of coming to camp back in those very early days, having only the bunkhouse, are no doubt as rich with memories as mine are. Their experiences occurred during an even simpler time with the focus even more on the pristine nature of that very special place.

Although carpentry was not my Uncle's line of work, he and his brother and sons built a solid and sturdy camp. It took them years to finish, doing it themselves, summers only while driving home to work each weekday.

Several years later they built Jack's camp, my Uncle's brother. My relation is to my Aunt but all of us, even my folks, have always called him "Uncle" Jack. Jack's wife, Dottie, was a wonderful woman, one who left a mark on a young girl growing up. She was diagnosed with Multiple Sclerosis when she was thirty years old. It was "tragic" my mother always said. She and Uncle Jack had not yet had children and Dottie loved them. Besides that, Dottie was a "career girl." She did not just have a job like my mother and many women in her generation and class, but she was rising in her profession and somehow more serious or devoted to it, I guess.

I always knew her to be in a wheel chair. Many times, I would watch my Uncle Jack's strong and vein-lined hands lift her lifeless legs from the chair into their car and back out. She never came down to the lake with the rest of us; perhaps my Uncle could not lift her all the way down the slippery hill or the wheelchair just could not make it down the steep incline over tree roots. Each time we would visit camp, my mother and I made a point to visit Dottie on her deck. I went by myself as I got older to enjoy the time I spent with her on my own. It was special for me.

Dottie was always so happy to see us. She was kind and cheerful, inquisitive and interesting, and she so loved company. Their camp was made accessible for her wheelchair. The relationships of both Uncle Jack and Dottie and Uncle Harold and Eileen left a solid impression on me of couples so dependent and caring of one another and always there to help the other in a calm, quiet, unpretentious way.

Their unions lasted their lifetimes, something that is very precious.

CHAPTER 11

How Our Days Looked

As we settle into a routine at home, to some degree, we did the same at camp. Although there was no pressure to do anything at any time at camp, our days had some similar happenings just because we, humans, are such habitual creatures.

When I awoke, I put on the pot of coffee and my robe and tiptoed outside without waking the guys. I walked all around the grounds and on the eastern side, I stopped to feel the intense heat of the morning summer sun on my face. It was so bright reflecting off the lake that I was forced to close my eyes. I basked in the quiet.

If there was a boat on the lake at that hour, its occupants fishing maybe, they could be speaking to one another in almost a whisper, but I was able to hear what they were saying as though I were in the boat with them. Voices carry on the lake in the early morning and in the evening.

I walked down to the dock and would look all around me. I sat on the planks, sometimes lifting my nightgown to dangle my feet over the side into the lake. Sometimes, I had to wipe a dewy spider web from the side before dipping my legs into the water. The lake was always cold at that time of the morning, even in the middle of July, and as calm and flat as a sheet of glass. I slipped my legs into the water so gently, trying not to make a ripple.

I love the early morning. Often, I saw fish swimming beside the dock. I sat quietly in an Adirondack chair for a few minutes, sipping my coffee, often giving gratitude for another new day in my life. All was so quiet. The sun would be slowly inching its way up in the sky – another glorious day beginning on a lazy summer day. It didn't get better than that. I felt so relaxed and calm.

In a song John Denver sings, he says she cried when she saw the sunshine. I never understood that; why would anyone cry? Alone, sitting on the dock in the morning or in the Adirondack chair at sunset as Frank and the boys headed off in the canoe to fish, I would just look at the brilliant light of the sun on the water, streaming through the gorgeous clouds, looking grayish as the sun began to set behind them, at a scene that made me so grateful for everything I had and everything I had right then. Giving gratitude in such a setting is almost automatic, takes no effort at all. It is this perhaps that could bring someone to tears.

By the time I went back inside the camp in the morning after my time spent walking around in my PJ's and sitting on the dock, the boys were usually up, already occupied with their own interests. Frank always stayed in bed a while and I would run down my offerings for breakfast to the boys.

Camp was as much about food as it was rest and relaxation. Easily, I spent three times what I normally did for a week's worth of groceries. There were too many potato chips for sure whenever company visited but for the most part, it was about good food. I love to cook and although it was hard to judge the heat of the stove which was slightly off-kilter, camp gave me the time to cook which I did not have enough of in my "real" life. Planning my evening meal at camp was all I had to do all day.

Breakfast was thick slices of cinnamon French toast, blueberry pancakes, or "Egg-Mc-Kalicky's." Ben had his egg scrambled (the rest of us, over-easy), sausage patty (Canadian bacon for me), a triangle slice of white American cheese (no cheese for Ben) on an English muffin (buttered for the boys).

July is strawberry season in Maine, and we always went to Maxwell's Farm in Cape Elizabeth to pick at least four quarts a day or so before we left for camp. I served strawberries at camp with every meal – sliced on breakfast plates with some blueberries; sliced on lunch plates with chunks of nectarine and grapes; mixed in a fruit salad of watermelon and blueberries for our late afternoon snack; in shortcake for our dessert after dinner. We love strawberries – ripe, red, juicy and sweet. They do not come any better than straight from the gardens of the Cape Elizabeth farm, which abuts the Atlantic Ocean. We cannot get enough of them and only get them local for the month of July.

Early August is blueberry season in Maine and late August raspberries bloom. In my husband's garden at home, his berries thrive and grow abundantly. Each year, it seems, we get more of a harvest than we did the year before. At peak season, his raspberries yield five bowls' worth every day all the way until October, nearly to the frost. He cuts the bushes right down at the end of each season so they bloom later than others' raspberries due to the need to grow up from tiny twigs over the course of the summer.

Grown fresh, they are radiant – firm, large, sweet. Ben would eat a bowl of raspberries each night himself. Only if you grow them can you eat them by the bowlful. Even in Maine, they can cost $5.00 for a half pint which equates to a handful and by the time they get to the grocer, they are already soft and get mushy quickly. Just like everything else in nature, there is nothing like the real thing in its true environment.

After I would get everyone started on breakfast, I pulled on my jogging clothes and took my run. If I were not afraid of dogs there would be no end to my exploring, but I am afraid. Twice bitten as a child, twice shy. I had to give the dogs the benefit – they were at camp in the country and if some intruder comes barreling down their dirt road, it only seemed fair that they could bark and growl and protect their spot. As someone who must be outside each day and yearns for wide-open spaces, I must roam. I cannot stay put. I also love to discover new things. Each time I headed out, I tried to find a new dirt road to check out.

Running at camp was the hardest running I'd ever done. I am a late bloomer when it comes to running; I took it up at thirty-six. My husband has been a runner all his life. One summer, after I had been running only one year, I coaxed him into running the Beach to Beacon 10k road race started in Cape Elizabeth, Maine by Olympic gold medalist of the first women's marathon, and native Mainer, Joan Benoit Samuelson.

I had to increase my runs from three and a half miles to six, which was a huge leap for me, a novice. I am much better running in the cold (the twenties seem to be my ideal running temperature) than the heat, and that summer was unbearably humid. It would hit me like a concrete wall and sock the life out of me. Remember, I am a Mainer with thick blood running through my veins to keep me warm through the winters.

Once I fainted in the shower from heat exhaustion; I lost a toenail; my weight vacillated as I tried to gage what was the adequate caloric intake for the energy I was expending. I never did figure it out and ended up gaining weight instead of losing it even when running six miles, four days per week. I could not skip running at camp due to our race deadline, which was coming shortly after our vacation.

The area in Raymond was so hilly; there was no relief. Not many cars came on the main route outside the camp road which I had to take to get the mileage, but those that did were coming very fast (one reason for the myriad of road kill each morning). As soon as I heard a car, I would have to lunge into the sand at the side of the road, and it was as deep as beach sand. The motions of running up and down hills and back and forth into the deep sand of the shoulder and then onto the curved pavement were a killer.

I did not wear my contact lenses when I ran early in the morning and the ground was littered with twigs. As I was just about to step on one, I discovered it was a black garden snake sunning himself on the hot blacktop. Panicked, I would have sprained my ankle before bringing my foot down on him!

One sweltering morning when Matt was maybe eight, I came running back down our camp road. He was sitting on the deck, playing. He got the biggest kick out of it when I did not stop at the camp but just kept right on running, right down the path to the lake, right out onto the dock and dove into the water, clothes, sneakers and all! It was such a relief. I'm lucky I didn't faint from having my body temperature so elevated and then plunging into that icy water.

Matt ran down after me. "Mom! Mom! What are you doing?!" Oh, he just thought it was hysterical. "Can I jump in too, Mom? Can I? With my clothes on?"

"Why not?" was my answer and in he jumped from the dock, laughing all the while.

After my morning exercise, Frank would have awoken and was ready to go fishing for a bit or kayaking, by himself. Although we are all social and can be quite charming when we want to, all four of us are introverts. Introverts are not necessarily wallflowers. It simply means that we get our strength and recharge our batteries by spending time alone. From an early age, Ben described his morning as "Ben time." (An extrovert, on the other hand, needs interaction and communication with others to recharge.) By each taking an hour alone in our day, we are more centered and then willing and able to be friendly and outgoing when around others for the rest of the day.

It took me no time to make the beds, clear away the breakfast dishes, sweep the floors, and clean the tiny bathroom. Cleaning at camp was minimal and quick and a nice change from the drudgery cleaning at home sometimes was.

Then we were down to the lake for the day. Sometimes we invited company or the boys' friends from back home. Sometimes friends just showed up. It was nice to have people every few days or so, not every day – again that break of being alone was so needed. Because both Frank and I worked full time, it was so important to us to spend our vacations together – just the four of us. There is no one I would choose over these three; my best times have been with them. It allowed us to have fun and focus on each other.

When the boys were small, I'd lay out a large blanket in the shade of a tree at the water's edge and line it with their toys and books. They'd have a shady play place all day. I'd place their child-size, plastic Adirondack chairs beside their blanket and sometimes they'd sit there and sometimes they'd move to their blanket, building with blocks or Lego's. Sometimes, they'd lay on their bellies reading their picture books. When Matt learned, he would read them to Ben as they lay side by side, Ben's face in his little hands as he lay on his belly listening to his big brother.

We took a boat ride each day around the lake; we swam together and lazily floated on the pillows and noodles while playing word games or "I spy" or "I'm thinking of a color that is...." or in later years, we began acting out skits based on the Drew Carey show "What's my line?" which was always great for some laughs. We kayaked. Matt and I had our own and Frank had the double for Ben to ride up front, the "minivan."

I preferred a kayak to a canoe. I liked the feeling of sitting right on the water, skimming across the lake and the waves like a water bug. I felt more "as one" with the lake and not so likely to tip. The kayak was small and easy for me to maneuver. I paddled close to the shoreline.

I kayaked to a sandy beach. Although I love the lake, sometimes, it could scare me. When the water was black and I couldn't see bottom, I wondered what swam below. Seeing *Jaws* as a teenager marked me and even in fresh water, I got a little creeped out thinking of the camera angles in the movie looking up from the depths at kicking legs at the surface.

When the water was clear and sometimes got very shallow, all of a sudden, I could see huge boulders inches below the surface and that would scare me, too. "Scare" may be too strong a word. Maybe "uneasy" would be a better word. I seemed to be becoming more uneasy as I aged, not less. I would think it would be the other way around having tried more and gained more experiences, and survived them, that would make me less scared, but that wasn't true in my case.

Sometimes, I found myself more timid than I liked and I would meditate on being "courageous" and having "no fear." I tried to talk myself through it asking what was the worst that could happen? And if it did happen, so what? At least I was trying and doing and living, and wasn't that more worthy of a pursuit than just observing from the sidelines? Observing can certainly bring me joy and pleasure and new experiences, but it never replaces the actual doing myself.

I once read that if you're not scared at least once every day, you're not being all you can be. You're living too much on the safe side, on the side that is known. Life is to live. It is to smell and feel and taste. Swim in the rain, in the dark under the moonlight even if you are afraid of water snakes. Feel what it's like to have your heart pump with adrenaline because you are a little scared or uneasy. Tube behind a very fast boat with the kids. What's the worst that can happen?

Well, I fell into the lake, and when my kids freeze framed the video and laughed hysterically at each bump of my ungraceful tumble into the waves, I laughed, too, at the pleasure we all got from my trying. It was pretty funny to watch. Sometimes, watching the video, veins popped out of my teenaged son's neck, he was laughing so hard, and hardy laughter like that was not something I saw often enough at that age. It made my fall into the lake from the tube so worth it.

Sometimes, when I was walking the grounds before breakfast and the boys were still asleep, I would take the kayak out myself in the cove. The lake was as smooth as glass and with the sun shining, I was able to see clear to the bottom, the sand, rocks, grass and the perch that blended in with the sand. I loved the quiet sound of the paddle parting the water and then coming out, dripping. There was something special about being up and out when the whole world was sleeping. It was a different world than I experienced in the day, with many sounds and bustle and people's voices. I found it both relaxing and stimulating.

The other time of day I tended to kayak was late afternoon. Around four or five o'clock to me was the golden hour – that magical time of day when the sun was dropping and the light became shimmery. The wind picked up across the dock and I'd have to put rocks on magazines and towels lying there. As the sun dropped in the sky and after I had had hours of swimming, sunning, reading and having fun, some wind down time again was welcome.

After one of our years at camp, when I returned to my office, I told my colleagues I had grown accustomed to a cold beer every day at four o'clock. Would that be a problem? I said I would like to replace that afternoon cappuccino I was in the habit of getting with a little stronger beverage. In a coffee cup, who would know? And wouldn't everyone appreciate my calm and carefree demeanor as we wound down our workday?

Somehow I knew a cold beer in a coffee cup at the office would never compare to that same cold beer drunk out of the glass bottle while sitting on the camp's dock, gazing out over the lake, the late afternoon sun shining off my sunglasses, my legs dangling in the water, listening only to birds and no human voices. No hurry, no worry, no problems, no crises. Only peace. There was truly no comparison.

Sitting in the sun would curb my appetite and I went almost all day with very little to eat. We liked tuna or chicken salad for lunch. I bought small, soft bulky rolls, hot ham and provolone at Micucci's, an old Italian market in downtown Portland. In my chicken salad, I included scallions or Bermuda onions chopped fine, grated carrots, almond slivers, celery and thyme. I drank many glasses of ice water all day, especially when it was hot. All of this contributed to needing very little to sustain me throughout the day.

We also loved fresh tomatoes with basil from the garden and mozzarella drizzled with olive oil. We spooned it onto slices of baguette which we'd buy from Standard Baking Company before leaving Portland. It was the most perfect snack or lunch. As a late afternoon snack, I also loved tapenade with pita crackers, especially with a glass of Pinot Noir.

I made a delicious gorgonzola spread for paninis. Into the food processor went gorgonzola, Dijon mustard, a little garlic, a little butter. It became like a paste. I spread it onto fresh sourdough slices of bread and topped it with shaved turkey and tomato or slices of cold filet mignon left over from the prior night's dinner with spinach. Either made the most scrumptious sandwich.

As the sun would start to drop, partly for the ambience of it, we would have our afternoon snack. When company was visiting, I would create a makeshift table down at the lake — our large Rubbermaid bucket where we kept our beach toys, turned upside down. I used the cover of the container as my serving tray to carry our wedge of cheddar, garlic & herb soft cheese, Havarti dill, Wheat Thins, maybe some home-made salsa and corn chips, or guacamole I made using the Barefoot Contessa's recipe.

We drank lemonade or iced tea which I made that morning by placing a large glass pitcher of ice water and six tea bags on the railing of the deck all day to brew, wine and wine glasses, grapes or triangle shaped pieces of watermelon. We used red checked napkins or Caspari florals and small paper plates. Dinner was a few hours off and this was such a nice, social pick-me-up.

Each evening after our dinner on the wooden picnic table, we walked down the camp road, each year a little further. It was all dependent on how far Ben could go and the longer walks marked his growing up. When the boys were young, Frank used to take them off road to follow along the side of a babbling brook where they claimed they saw bear tracks. Some summers there was not much babbling, just a dry riverbed.

I loved the camp road. It was a true camp road, unpaved part of the way, thickly-leaved trees crowning over it. The camps were not too close to one another. In between the camps, we could view the lake as we walked. Camp owners had fire pits and Adirondack chairs, painted dark green or pastel colors like sky blue or pale yellow set permanently on their lawns for company.

About mid-way down the road, we could see an island with one camp on it. An elderly man lived there. He maintained the green grass and flowers beautifully; all of the island and his camp were neat and orderly. He had a "party barge" and a small sailboat. He also had a golf cart to take his load of supplies from the lake up the hill to his camp. To get to his island, there was a sandbar from our side of the land to it. Each time we kayaked, the boys always wanted to get out on the sandbar. It was so inviting.

But it still gave me a sick feeling. The first year we came to camp, I could not even canoe over it and nearly held my breath when Frank slowly drove our aluminum boat over it. Not all my camp memories are pleasant.

When I was about seven, my cousin used to take me to her friend's camp down the road, one that looked right down onto the sandbar and across to the island. On one particular evening, the teenage girls had been making me up, admiring my long eyelashes and brushing my hair. All of a sudden there was pandemonium and shouting. We ran out front with the girl's parents onto the concrete stairs leading down to the lake. I cannot recall seeing anything. I just remember the shouting and the chaos. My cousin, Corliss, stood behind me, one stair above, and I believe she must have put her hands over my eyes as we stood on the steps, high above the sandbar.

A teenage boy drowned right in front of us on the sandbar. It seemed so strange that it could happen in two feet of water. Evidently, his foot got tangled in a root on one of the deep sides of the sandbar. Sandbars are odd in that they are sandy and shallow but on either side, the lake generally drops off fast over your head and is very black.

Although he was a teenager and a strong swimmer, a freak accident took his life and the men who waded out quickly to save him were too late. Even the doctor a few camps away was called down in the panic but the boy was already dead by the time he arrived.

The story I have just shared is as clear to me as if it happened yesterday. It had lain dormant for many years; coming back to camp and riding over the sandbar reminded me of it.

Over the years we returned to camp, it began to dim for me…or maybe not dim….I just acknowledged that it happened in my past and I put it away.

CHAPTER 12

Perch City

Frank took the boys fishing in the small, aluminum boat with an eight-horse power motor. Our lawn mower motor at home was bigger. When they were young, they would sit at attention wearing tight orange life jackets, the wind from the slow ride gently blowing their hair. Sometimes Ben would sit in the bow. He was so small, he looked the way a puppy does eagerly sitting up front feeling the breeze.

They went to a spot around the point, in the cove on the inside of the island, which they named "Perch City." Every time they dropped their lines, they caught a small perch. When the boys' friends came up, they always got to go to "Perch City." Grown-ups sometimes worry that a first fishing trip will yield no results and the kids will become bored with it. Oh, they were lucky if their first fishing trip was while visiting us at camp.

When Ben's little friend, Keegan, visited him at age five, after twenty fish apiece, Frank figured that was enough! Ben had a small fishing pole about two feet long with a Snoopy bobber on the end. Of course, Matt had to say, "Hey, Ben! Look at Snoopy! He's doing the dead-dog float!" as Snoopy floated nose down marking the spot where the line went in.

Off the dock after dark, two foot-long bass were caught — one by Frank and one by Matt, fortunately. Oh, there was much excitement in pulling those babies up. Yes, there were certainly fish in Crescent Lake….and then the fishing excursions took on a new sense of excitement. (I have been told other lakes are "fished out" when no one has luck pulling one in.) Now that they got a feel for the excitement of true weight on the line (not a "leaf fish" or a "stick fish"), going fishing became that much more alluring.

At the end of the lake was a metal tunnel called Tenney Tunnel under the road leading to a small river, which in turn emptied into the next lake. It was "Fish Haven" down that river — snapping turtles sunning themselves on fallen logs, beaver dams, frogs and water lilies, grass growing up through the water, woods on both sides of the river. Boats traveled very slowly through the river, and boaters waved and nodded to one another as they passed.

The water lilies were so beautiful from a distance, but when I picked one, they were not pretty at all. They were filled with bugs and died quickly. They were made to live, in water, not to be ripped off their underwater stems. Water lilies, like all wild flowers, are prettier if left in their natural environment; they are not meant to be ripped from it and brought to places unnatural and so die quickly.

When we slowed down to a crawl to go through the shallow tunnel under the road which led into the river, I would begin a chorus of "Row, row, row your boat" hoping the others would come in, in turn. Ben had another idea. He screamed at the top of his voice, high pitched and obnoxious, echoing off the metal, and then burst out laughing at the end of the tunnel.

CHAPTER 13

I Don't Like Spiders & Snakes

When we invited the boys' friends to stay with us, we made it a true camp experience. When they were young, we'd drive to town, pick up the friends, bring them back to camp for a day of sun, swimming, playing horseshoes, rock painting, and burgers, corn on the cob, and strawberry shortcake or blueberry pie á la mode on the picnic table for dinner. Then, we'd make s'mores over the campfire after dark and drive them back to town. Sometimes, they'd all be asleep within fifteen minutes of leaving camp after such an exhausting day outdoors.

When the boys became teenagers, we'd invite the friends for an overnight. They'd sleep in the tent on cots down on the point by the water. We'd see their lantern on until the time we turned in ourselves — the boys playing Gameboy, watching a DVD on their laptop or maybe even telling a ghost story or two.

After so much adventure, I was disheartened one year when I dropped Billy off in his driveway and when his Mom came out to greet us, the first thing he uttered was, "I had a leech on me! I had a leech on me!" Early in the day, he had a small leech, no bigger than a half inch and skinny on his shin. He didn't freak out at the lake; he let me get the salt and take care of it calmly, but his bellowing it out to his Mom the second he got out of our car showed me it was more of a big deal to him than he had showed us earlier.

Well, Billy had no idea that a tiny leech one year would lead to a giant snake another! And to think he was panicked at the tiny leech!

It was a gorgeous day and my parents and in-laws were visiting as was Ben's friend Billy. Ben and Billy were swimming; a couple of us sat on the dock; my in-laws sat in the Adirondack chairs on the sunny spot at the top of the dock. Someone said, "Hey, what's that?" We all looked in the direction they were pointing.

A little dark something was bobbing along the water about twenty feet out from the dock. We looked at it casually and wondered, "Is it a turtle?" "Is that a turtle head?"

As it continued to come closer to the dock, we speculated as to whether it was simply a stick floating along the current. My in-laws came down onto the dock to see what we were all looking at as did my parents and then Frank. The bobbing thing came within three feet of the dock and it wasn't a turtle. It was about a three or four foot long red and tan striped snake swimming in the water with its head outside!

We freaked. The snake was so brazen as to continue to come closer to us; he wasn't frightened in the least. Now Billy and Ben ran out of the water and up onto the dock. With so many of us on the dock, it began to sink. We were screaming and jumping up and down; we couldn't believe it was a snake. It was so gross! As if the mayhem wasn't enough, the sinking of the dock caused an even worse situation…..the dock spiders from underneath all began to crawl up onto the dock. And dock spiders are huge!

Year to year, I didn't really think about creepy crawly things living under the dock where I sat and dozed so peacefully, but these giant critters scrambling up onto the top boards so as not to be drowned freaked me out. Just like in a movie, they came scrambling up from all sides, heading toward the middle of the dock all at the same time…where we were all crowded. We all went running up the ramp to the lawn, screaming more and flailing our arms. What pandemonium!

Frank jumped quickly into a kayak and drove the snake out deeper by smashing the paddle down onto the water close to the snake to frighten him and get him to move in the direction Frank wanted. When he returned, Frank got all his cans of Raid and saturated the dock spiders.

He continued to spray Raid on the dock every morning for the rest of that week trying to protect us from witnessing any more. So much for clean air; the toxins of the Raid probably polluted us for years.

For the entire week thereafter, while on the float at different spots on the lake, I'd see a small black ball floating along. When the ball came closer, I would find it was a dead dock spider all curled up in death from being poisoned by Raid.

It was actually lucky my parents and in-laws were visiting that day because years' worth of positive camp experiences could have been totally wiped out for me. Instead, my Mom and father-in-law changed the subject, got into the lake, and took a swim. My Mom floated along in a big black inner tube, calm as could be. Ben and Billy watched them from the beach. I watched all of them from afar. Tentatively, in time, Ben and Billy got back in. Not me, not yet.

I may never have stepped foot back into the lake all that week if Mom and my father-in-law hadn't broken the ice for us. They just laughed at the comedy of the entire scene; chalked it up to living in nature; and went back to enjoying the sunshine and cool water. I couldn't relax for the rest of the week. I wouldn't sit on the dock except when the boys were taking a swim. I wore my sunglasses and sat like a navy officer surveying back and forth across the water line, so hopeful snakes had to keep their heads above water to breathe so I could see them coming.

When Billy was brought home that day, oh what a story he had to tell. Made the leech look like child's play. I'm not sure if his parents believed the extent of the snake story — the drama and comedy of it seemed too much to be real. Amazingly, Billy came back to visit us every year. And, yes, we continued to return ourselves, every year. Camp and living in nature once in a while have made us more hardy than we might otherwise be.

Chapter 14

The General Store

Usually once or maybe twice during our stay, sometimes on a rainy day if we were looking for time to kill, we took the boys down to the general store down the main route a-ways. That store took us back in time. The storefront was built on the front of the white farmhouse where the owners lived.

There was a dirt spot out front where one car could pull up; otherwise, we had to park in the owners' driveway. The store had a wooden farmer's porch on the front with a bulletin board tacked up on the clapboards with notices of town news, missing pets, bean suppers and other upcoming events. On the left side of the porch were bundles of wood tied together with twine and a handwritten sign on a piece of a cardboard box in black magic marker that said "Campfire Wood $2.50 a bundle."

On the right side of the porch was an old bench with its green paint chipping off. Above it in the window, from the inside, on a white piece of paper, not a cardboard box, there was another handwritten but apparently more permanent sign that said:

Fishing licenses

Worms

Whoppie pies

There was an ancient, rusted Coca Cola bottle/thermometer nailed beside the doorframe. On one of the posts beside the stairs, a flag waved in the breeze saying OPEN when they were. Inside, the wood floors creaked and there were glass cases with dark wood corner panels holding the goods. They looked like old pharmacy cases. The glass of the cases was very thick. There was one gray metal shelf dividing two aisles with small can and dry goods — not the family size boxes but all in miniature, just enough to get us by until we could get to the supermarket. The boxes reminded me of the groceries that come with children's play kitchen sets. There were boxes of cereal, cans of tuna, band aids, toilet tissue.

Most of the merchandise was within or on top of the glass cases. At one end of the store was the "penny" candy which had increased in price from twenty-five cents to a dollar each. They had the candy of old: wax bottles to chew and drink the juice out of; hot balls, "fiery hot;" Mary Janes; gum cigarettes (believe it or not), tootsie rolls; and then some new candy: sour patch kids; ring pops; baby bottle pops, cowtails, gummy bears.

When they were younger, this is why my boys loved to visit. They selected several pieces of candy and put them in their own tiny paper bags, and a bagful of what they chose was generally no more than $1.50. I was amazed at the joy such a small cost could grant to children as they held their little bags tightly in their small hands.

Newspapers and plain brown paper bags were on the counter beside a giant, tarnished gold and gilded cash register with push down buttons. The register must have weighed three hundred pounds and had to be one hundred years old. It did not give a receipt. It just added up our scant purchases and housed the bills and coins. The owner counted back your change; the register didn't do the tally.

For newspapers, we had our pick of the *Portland Press Herald* or the *Portland Press Herald*. No *New York Times* or *Boston Globe* here even though most owners on our camp road lived out-of-state throughout New England and would probably have purchased them if they were available.

Away At A Camp In Maine

If someone didn't have their wallet, I saw a woman once write down her purchase, a yogurt, on a paper bag and tell the owner she would bring the money in next time. The owner said no sweat...just write it down. She replied, "I don't even know the cost. I'll just write 'yogurt' and catch you next time I'm in. Thanks a mill!"

CHAPTER 15

Running the Camp Roads

Out on the main route, a quarter mile north of the camp road, was a yellow farmhouse that I used to dream about. I discovered it on one of my morning runs. You would probably find it plain and maybe old, but it was everything I love. I'm a romantic and I love old, especially when it comes to homes. Originally, the house may have been one floor. It looked like it began as a small square abode with a slab of gray stone as its front stoop and a half-moon shaped dirt driveway out front.

Inside the half moon driveway stood an ancient tree. It was a perfect tree. Its trunk was gray and weathered, rough and wide, with lumps like tumors on it. I could not wrap my arms around it; that's how wide it was. Its full green leaves in summer were perfectly rounded and crowned so high above the house. This tree had stood on this spot for many, many years. It shaded the front lawn of the house.

The square portion of the house was two stories high but the second floor clearly looked newer than the first. It blended nicely with the look of the farmhouse, but its windows appeared newer.

To the left of this main portion of the home was a long section of the house, one floor, which was probably also added some years later. The kitchen was now in this lengthy portion and what a cozy kitchen I imagined it to be – wide pine board floors throughout, low beamed ceilings, a gray, stone fireplace as high as my shoulders with a black, cast iron pot hanging decoratively over the fire. The gray chandelier over the thick, rectangular oak table, in my mind, was Shaker style and had candles in it instead of light bulbs.

The entire backside of this portion of the house was small-paned glass doors and the morning sunlight streamed in across the house. When I ran by the front in the early mornings, I saw the reflection of that backyard light pouring through the house from the back and out the front windows.

I'm sure the rooms were small and cut up, as houses were made in years past. There were probably built-in bookshelves and hutches and the moldings were no doubt wide and ample. Although I never set foot on their wood floors, I am sure they creaked.

I imagined rolling pie crust with an old wooden rolling pin on their butcher block counter tops, flour tossed haphazardly to keep the dough from sticking; heaping colanders of ripe berries freshly picked from their gardens on the sideboard waiting to fill my pies.

I imagined the smells of roasting turkey and bread baking. Can you not see the plump red tomatoes, dripping wet from just being rinsed in the old white porcelain farmhouse sink, and leafy green lettuce waiting to be tossed into the wooden salad bowl? If you were from another planet, you would know that produce picked from a garden for salad was good for you. No language would need to be spoken. The colors of things in nature are so vivid and nothing man-made will ever capture their brilliance. Is anything outside nature as captivating as a plump orange pumpkin in autumn?

I imagined the warmth of their woodstove in winter and could see a fire blazing in their small front room fireplace whose hearth was not raised from the wood floor but instead was comprised of bricks inlaid one foot around the fireplace, up against the hard wood flooring. In my mind's eye, I heard the crackle of the fire and saw the occasional log fall from its perch, sending ashes dancing into the air.

Further to the left of this lengthy kitchen addition was an enormous attached barn. Besides the overflowing window boxes on all the windows across the front of the house, the barn was what captured my attention and drew me to this house. I am attracted to barns. In my office, I have two photographs I shot of two different barns – both red with white trim, one set beside a bright yellow house. I like their clean lines, particularly Shaker-style, and love when they're ancient.

The dirt and grass drive leading from this barn to the half moon driveway was a ramp built up from the earth. On either side of the ramp were hand packed gray stones. Below the kitchen addition and beside the ramp leading to the barn was an old-fashioned double, bead board, set of dark green doors probably leading to a cellar or storage spot beneath the kitchen.

Flowers abounded all across the front of the house – ferns, orange tiger lilies, lupines, black-eyed Susans – growing tall and wild. The window boxes were filled with purple, yellow and pink pansies and geraniums with ivy streaming down toward the grass. Terra cotta pots were scattered randomly across the side lawn overflowing with more flowers. The tenants were gardeners. They cared lovingly for their yard.

There was a curved dirt road to the left of the barn, overhung with more full trees and shoots of yellow grass like wheat blowing softly in the breeze. While running down that road, behind this house, I discovered the expanse of it and its barn.

The side of the barn was painted red and the back was shingled with a natural, weathered stain. Behind the barn were several acres of meadows and eventually woods. At different times during the seasons, they mowed and baled the hay after it dried sufficiently. The large rolls of hay were sometimes scattered throughout the meadows waiting to be picked up and brought to the barn. Hand packed stone walls marked their property lines.

In back of the house, behind the kitchen was a gray stone patio, again, overflowing with pots of plants and a stone fireplace. The fireplace was covered with ferns, unused. There was a gazebo-like birdhouse atop a tall silver pole just beside the patio. A myriad of birds flittered and flew in and out of it. It was seeing the expanse of the house, front and back, that captivated me and stirred a certain mood in me, a comfortable feeling of hominess.

You may wonder how I know so much of the house if I have never stepped foot inside. Our last summer renting, my beautiful farmhouse was empty. At first running by, I didn't realize it. But then it was the flowers that alerted me. They were not tended to that year as they had been in past years; the window boxes were not filled. The little forest green Jetta was not parked in the half moon drive. My farmhouse tenants, whom I never knew, had left.

I felt like I knew them. I felt like I knew their life – their morning coffee on the patio, their afternoons in winter reading in a rocker by their enormous kitchen fireplace, their quiet summer bedtimes hearing only crickets chirping in their meadows.

I had to peek in the windows of the empty house and all I saw did not disappoint me. It was as I was imagining. They would never know that I had photographed their charming house and had pictures hanging in my living room at home. Many guests comment to me on these photos. One is the pale yellow house, in summer, the glorious flowers. The second piece is two photos within the same frame. One photo is a path marked in one of the meadows toward the back of their property where a truck drove across it. The second photo within the frame is another ancient tree which stands beside that path. It looks similar to the old tree inside the half moon drive. The leaves on the tree are beautiful in my summer photo.

I took these photos several summers back to remind me – remind me of camp, remind me of summer, remind me of the peace and solitude I enjoyed when running those paths alone each year.

When I found the tenants gone, peeking into the barn was even more of a draw than the house. There was a small rectangle cut into the fifteen-foot doors near where a door handle or pull might have been at one time. I bent down, sweating from my run on the warm summer morning, and put my face close to the cutout.

The smell of the barn and the heat from it wafted through. It transformed me to Charlotte's barn. I half expected to see Wilbur the pig and the Goosey Gander stuttering across the worn board floor with her little goslings behind her. The barn was so tall, completely open down the center to the rafters. On either side, was a loft complete with bales of hay. Below the loft on the left side were stalls, probably homes to horses in years passed. There was a black Wilson punching bag hanging toward the front and an old wooden kitchen chair, its cane seat ripped.

A thick rope hung from the loft, maybe to pull up the bales. Sunlight streamed through a small, dirty glass window up toward the roofline in the back. Oh how I wanted to go inside but the door was locked. I felt the stillness of it, the musty, hot hay smell and knew I was trespassing into someone else's life.

There were names carved into the molding on the side of the barn door but I couldn't read them. As I ran away, I wondered if there were children. I thought about the owners and wondered where they had all gone. Quietly, to myself, I said good bye to them; something else at camp that I needed to now acknowledge for the pleasure it had given me. Like a photo, I tried to solidify it in my mind, and then I had to wish them well and say "So long. All the best. And thanks for what your home has given to me."

Chapter 16

Thunderstorms on the Lake

Weather on the lake was so much more intense than it was in the city. I'm not sure if it seemed this way simply because my vision was unimpaired and I had the time to actually look at it, really watch it, or if it was truly stronger weather.

The expanse of an open lake, a kind of valley within a ring of trees and mountains circling it, seemed to give room for the different types of weather to stretch and dominate the entire area. Perhaps without the broken horizon from neighborhood houses or roads, it allowed the rain to splash down unencumbered and therefore harder and more visual.

It poured on the lake. It did not simply shower. Rain came down so hard it looked like hail. Or it was hail... even in July. At times, we would be in the midst of a heavy rain and yet saw the sun shining and no rain at the far end of the lake. Sometimes, we actually saw a storm coming our way, starting the rain at one end of the lake and then watching it come across the water until it reached, and soaked, us.

After a heavy and quick afternoon rain, sometimes we saw enormous rainbows stretched across our lake, end to end, when the sun returned.

I have seen huge cumulous clouds that must have stretched for miles in the sky. After a strong rain, the sky could be bright royal blue, the clouds pure white and puffy. Sometimes the sun was behind the clouds and it shined its rays making the cloud kind of translucent. The sun shining through a crack in the clouds in that way was God to me.

Sometimes when hiking, I'd see these rays shine through the treetops in this way and brighten my path. When I saw this sight, I couldn't help but sigh and be inspired by things bigger than me and beyond my capacity to understand. I always felt tiny at this sight and in awe of all that nature had to offer. There is no man-made equivalent to the beauty and colors in nature.

I have seen small puffs of fog, which appeared like smoke, hovering at the tops of the trees, spotted here and there along the eastern side of the lake across from me. I have seen white capped waves start out of seemingly nothing in the middle of the lake, head toward the shore, but fizzle out well before. I have seen a lake as flat and smooth as glass and one that looks as choppy and windswept as the ocean.

One summer afternoon, the sky grew increasingly gray. A storm was on its way. Suddenly, the clouds seemed to come all the way down within feet of the lake. They were gray/white and wispy like smoke. They enveloped our section of the lake. I was in the camp and Frank called me down to the dock excitedly. He had grabbed his camera. "Come, quick! Look at this!"

When I got to the dock, I was amazed. All was totally quiet and I was immediately reminiscent of the movie *Close Encounters of the Third Kind*. The sky looked like nothing I had ever seen before. The clouds didn't look like clouds but smoke and they were lingering so close to our heads, hiding the other side of the lake. The quiet, the stillness, the gray/white – it was a sight like I had never seen swirling around me. I stayed for only a few minutes and then ran back up to the camp. In minutes, it began to downpour, thunder clapped loudly right overhead.

Thunderstorms on the lake were intense. On occasion we had one during an afternoon but it seemed most often they began deep in the night when we were sound asleep. We always left the windows open when we slept. Occasionally, the sound of rain pouring on the roof shingles would awaken us but if that didn't do it in a soothing manner, the first clap of thunder, usually right overhead, surely would.

The claps seemed louder on the lake and even I, who loved the coziness of thunderstorms — being safe inside, listening only and not participating — and the thrill of them, was afraid to hear them in the night at camp. It sounded like the camp roof would rip right off.

How could the lightening, which cut through the dark in a jagged line all the way down to the lake, not hit our small camp or one of the many trees towering over our roof? Maybe it was partly the dark of camp at night, no streetlamps or lights burning in nearby camps, so the lightening was so much brighter. Maybe it was the lack of insulation of the camp which made me feel like I was within the storm, right in its belly, anticipating nervously whatever outcome it would bring.

I recall one storm that began with heat lightening. Just as we were getting into our beds, we began to see the flashes of light, quick, almost undistinguishable. We were talking about our day and our plans for tomorrow, safe inside the camp and barely noticing the blackness of night outside.

We probably didn't notice the lightening until several minutes from when it began. There was not a sound.

Frank ran outside to view it. He was so impressed by its power, its magnitude flashing across the lake, in the valley of the mountains. He stood at the water's edge just observing. All of a sudden, he heard it in the distance - the rumbling of thunder coming our way across the lake. I was lying in our bed, frightened just a bit. I was able to lie in bed and look onto the lake through the front picture window. I thought it was the wind rustling the leaves; the sound was growing intense, but then Frank came bolting through the great room door, laughing, shaking his wet hands at his sides, slipping as he pushed through the door. It was not the leaves making that sound; it was down pouring.

Then the fury of the thunder storm hit us. For nearly thirty minutes, it settled right over our camp, the huge lightening bolts coming from as high up in the sky as we could see before black blocked out everything. Storms on a lake are so loud, so physical, so awe inspiring and you feel so tiny in their midst, so insignificant. The thunder split the night right overhead and lightening lit up the entire cottage each time it cracked. The bolts were broad but jagged like in pictures and came straight down from the heavens right to the lake, splitting the sky.

As I lay in our bed, my faced turned away from the lake, I held tight to my quilt and prayed for safety. That cottage had been built so many years ago; I told myself that was certainly not going to be the night it would be struck and burn to the ground.

Amazingly, the boys never woke in the night, even Matt sleeping so high in the rafters with the claps seemingly inches from his head. It was the peace of childish sleep, nothing to fear and nothing weighing on their minds. They slumbered through the night and woke to the grounds strewn with branches and wet fallen leaves and the sun coming up over the eastern point as it did every morning. The smell of the soaked pine needles and bushes was fresh.

Thunder storms on the lake forced me to take notice of nature, made me realize how small and insignificant humans are. We are ants. As the wind whips through trees, hundreds of years old, with trunks nearly three feet in diameter and yet bending under the wind's raw power, almost screaming from the beating their branches were taking, while white capped waves pounded the shore, we saw how powerful nature is. Nothing man made is as powerful. Man has built weapons to destroy and maim, but nature can wipe out more, quicker, and then the earth heals and mends itself. Trees grow back. Bushes grow back, and plants; waves subside. Man can destroy, but what he has created will not heal and mend, will not renew itself.

Just before the storm began, we looked at the orange crescent moon. *Red sky at night, sailor's delight* is how the saying goes. Red sky at night tells us we will have another beautiful day tomorrow on the lake.

"Rain in the night, Mom?" the boys asked casually the next morning.

"Yes," I replied and shivered the tiniest little tremble. "A bit." The ordeal of a thunderstorm passed again and left us safe; no need for more words than that.

CHAPTER 17

The Children's Camp

There were three children's camps on Crescent Lake. When I was young, they were segregated as "girls" or "boys" camps but didn't seem to be any longer. When we rode past their beaches in our aluminum boat, I saw both boys and girls running and swimming.

One camp was diagonally across the lake from our dock. When I was having my morning quiet time down by the water, I heard the children awakened to *Revelry* played on a bugle. Perhaps they were still asleep at that hour and it woke them….if the sleepover from the night before was boisterous and late….or maybe they had been up for a long time as I had. Perhaps it was simply their call to breakfast.

Groups of the campers, a dozen or so of them at a time, came out onto the lake in their small, white day sailors. From my distance, they looked like little toy sailboats floating around my son's bath when he was a baby. They sailed in no particular direction, in and out, back and forth. Up close, they must have kept a safe distance from one another but from my vantage point, they looked like a collection of random boats on a potential collision course.

After thirty to forty-five minutes, a horn signaled the boaters it was time to bring them in. Like automatons, they all turned their little crafts toward the shore and made their way to the beach.

They canoed in matching red boats and water-skied amongst a path of pylons the counselors lined up lengthwise toward the side of the lake each morning. Their days were filled with organized water sports.

Their beach was pure white sand; the lake marked with white buoys as swimming areas with a raft. On the beach were wooden racks of flotation devices, oars, kickboards, all neatly lined up and put away after each excursion. Their rec hall was way up the hill to the left of the beach. It was a long, natural colored log building with a green tin roof. It was completely encased with pines, elms and birches.

At 9:00 p.m. each night, the call to bed brought the campers to the close of another fun and fulfilling day on the lake. The call, just like at wake-up, was played on the bugle – *Taps*, slow and final. Frank was normally having his quiet evening time down by the lake and listened to that song with a heavy heart...the close of another wonderful day at camp, the passing of day into night and back into day.

The peace of this order and ritual was so relaxing. That's all it's about. Life is so sweet. Everything he could want and everyone he wanted to be with were there with him. He would not feel guilty for wanting only this and nothing and no one more. This pace and the passing of his days allowed him to stop and realize what really mattered to him and what was really important to him. And to me.

CHAPTER 18

Annual Lobster Feed

Even as Mainers, we only eat lobster once or twice each summer. A good friend of mine, Terena, had in-laws who owned lobsterpots as more of a hobby than a business. Terena therefore ate lobster almost every week; she grew sick of it. When her daughter, Kea, was six, she painted her own buoy, pink with a purple stripe, and set a trap of her own. Each family paints their own buoys with a design unique to them.

Lobstering is regulated and territorial in Maine; it is the livelihood of many living on the coastline. We used to get invited to my friend's home to ice skate in winter and were served hot chocolate, Earl Grey tea and steaming mugs of rich, lobster stew. When they visited us at camp, they brought us lobster salad with mayonnaise, celery, macaroni and large chunks of white lobster meat.

At the rehearsal dinner for their wedding, they had a traditional lobster bake on the ocean at Winslow Park in Freeport. Frank loves lobster and does not get it as much as he'd like. There was a large freezer sized storage container filled with cooked lobster for the wedding party. I am sure Frank ate at least eight lobsters that night. His eyes were brimming; he had never seen so many lobsters in his life and he just could not stop eating them. After the steamed clams, thick clam chowder, and corn on the cob steamed in the fire under pounds of seaweed, eight lobsters is just too much before a heaping bowl of strawberry shortcake on homemade biscuits.

My friend and her husband ate boiled lobster, lobster rolls, lobster over linguini, lobster quiche. They were known to eat lobster for breakfast.

So our minimal lobster feed one or two times each summer is not exemplary of a "true" Mainer…..but we do have to have at least one meal of it each summer. We would never order lobster in a restaurant. It is a delicacy and pricey but in restaurants, it is downright ridiculous.

It is also too messy to eat out. Generally, we have the supermarket steam them for us and pick them up all cooked, the smell of cooking them is intense and lingers in our house for days.

At camp, we boiled them ourselves with all the windows open wide to emit the smell. When I was young, I did not eat lobster but my parents did, again once or twice each summer like we do. You must purchase and cook lobsters alive. I recall being in New York City on business one August, three months pregnant and nauseous. A few colleagues and I walked through Chinatown one hot, late afternoon beginning to think of dinner. The heat and smells of the city in summer were overpowering to a newly pregnant woman in the throes of morning sickness. At a corner market, I swore they were selling dead lobsters. My friends tried to calm me saying surely they were alive….just not moving. I still think they were dead - a big no-no for lobsters. And I believe I ate broth that night for dinner, all I could stomach.

When I was a kid, my parents would get the large lobster pot of water boiling rapidly and then take the creatures out of their insulated bags and let them crawl on our kitchen floor. They are dark greenish-black before they are cooked. They are tough looking critters, banged up. Sometimes one is missing a claw, probably from a fight. Their shells are usually marked and scarred. The fish markets put rubber bands around their claws so they can't snap your fingers. My parents thought it was funny I guess to let them crawl around. I was afraid of them.

I would scooch down on a kitchen chair, not letting my toes anywhere near the floor. Then my Dad would pick them up one at a time, make some parting comment to them, and with mittened hands, he would drop them into the boiling water. How barbaric is that? You can see why as a child I would not eat them. Even if the meat was sweet and juicy and unlike any type of fish or shellfish, they became more like pets crawling around my kitchen floor. I am a city girl and do not kill my food to eat it; I buy it nicely packaged from the supermarket.

Then, after the initial violence of killing and boiling them alive, eating them is just as barbaric. They are served whole, still in their shell, head and all, on your plate, bright orange-red and hot. You must rip them apart to eat them, boiling water pouring out as you tear each appendage of its body apart.

Depending on the season and whether they are soft shell or hard, we may need nutcrackers to break the shell and then use pokers to get the meat out. At camp, we each had a small bowl of melted butter beside our plates. I dipped my pieces of meat in one at a time and ate them. My Dad completely cleaned his lobster and put all the meat into his small bowl to soak in the butter. He would do that for two or three lobsters. Then he comfortably sat back and indulged himself, one piece of buttery meat at a time.

I ate only the claws and tail but I have been with some folks who eat every bit of the lobster. They suck the juices out of all their tiny legs; they eat the body including the green tomalley and roe.

We always needed a large bowl on the table for the refuse. It was generally a shared bowl and as lobster juice or butter dripped down our chins, our hands and fingernails soaked and dirty from the manual work of conquering our dinner, the hot smell in the kitchen from the steaming pot, and summertime conversation, we tossed our shells into the community bowl and once it was filled, we'd empty it into the trash and begin again. In restaurants, they serve bibs when you order a lobster.

Lobster is a delicacy and eating it like no other experience. Lobster signifies summer in Maine. Business outings, family reunions, and sometimes summer weddings on the shoreline will serve this traditional Maine feast. With the tradition of coming to camp each summer came our annual lobster feed. I did not let them crawl around the floor first - didn't want to traumatize my boys - but still they did not eat lobster. As children, they preferred a bowl of pasta with butter, grated Romano and a slice of garlic toast on the side, but now as young men, the lobster ravioli at Paciarino in Portland lures them, and they've come into their native Maine heritage.

CHAPTER 19

Hiking to the Summit

Across the main route, outside Fire Road 231 that was our camp road, was Rattlesnake Mountain. It was privately owned, but the sign on the fence welcomed visitors. It asked us to respect the property and leave it as we found it. It was offered to the public for their pleasure and was maintained by the family who owned it.

There was a small wooden box beside the fence where we could park our car and begin our walk. Atop the box were walking sticks of all lengths left by climbers before us, to share with those coming after.

The climb to the summit was an easy half-mile, suited for beginners. It started as a fairly wide path and then turned into stairs of rocks by the end. The boys could easily do the hike from when they were quite young. In June, I saw lady slippers beside the path. Chipmunks were everywhere, chasing after us as we walked, as though tame.

Sometimes we came to the mountain even when we were not staying at the camp, just for the hike. The view from the summit was beautiful. It overlooked our small lake and another one beyond. We identified the point where our camp was located although we were unable to see it through the trees; the bright yellow and navy water trampoline across the lake from our camp; "Perch City" and the sandbar where we kayaked that morning. We nibbled trail mix that we made ourselves; Ben scoffing most of the M&M's out of the mixture for himself.

We sat on the flat rock on the summit and looked down for several minutes, sometimes for a half hour or so. While we sat, Matt took each footpath from the rock, one leading to the back of the mountain, one leading down the front, one parallel to the trail we just hiked. He explored for a few minutes down each path, coming back to us on the rock after each, using his walking stick as though he needed it. The breeze blew up the face of the mountain and softly dried our sweaty faces. When the M&M's were gone, Ben was ready to head back down. Hike was over.

CHAPTER 20

"Snogs"

Birch trees were an anomaly amongst all the dark grayish black trunks. Their peeling white bark with black markings, peach/pink on its underside, and small light green leaves at the very top, were such a contrast to the heavy pines and oaks. The trunks of the birches were thin, tall and crooked. They were more frail than the other trees. They dotted the campground in amongst the more hardy trees and surrounded the lake.

My Maid of Honor, Sally, collected a basket of pinecones when she visited and small acorns. The double acorns attached at their caps reminded us of Siamese twins.

She wanted to take something natural as a reminder of her weekend and put it on her desk at Boston College, to remind her of what the world outside work was like, outside in the woods, away, the peace and joy and relaxation she felt.

The lake bottom was rocky near the dock. Because our boys had come to camp since they were young, they did not mind the rocks or the muck out deeper. Nor did they mind the occasional strands of grass growing just off the beaten swimming area. We did not need water shoes; we were used to it.

Water shoes have only come out in the last several years. I think my relatives were the original makers of water shoes although they never patented the design. They knew forty years ago that for some, barefoot on rocks and a little squishy muck was not as pleasant as it could be so they would save their old white basketball or tennis sneakers, the Converse ones with the plain red stripe down the side. They would break down the back of the sneaker so they could slip their foot in the back, kind of like a flipper, kind of like a clog.

My friend, Al, had a name for them - "snogs" - you know a sneaker/clog, interestingly the design of the Crocs that have become so popular. The snogs would bleach even whiter from year after year in water and air drying in the sunshine on the dock.

We had friends visit who owned beautiful pools in suburbia. Their children didn't quite know what to do at the lake; they were not used to anything except smooth, clean plastic against their tiny toes. Some adapted and instantly got into the camp groove; some did not. It was always interesting to me to see how quickly they adapted. It was those who did that I knew would crave getaways in nature like this when they grew older. It was those who did not that didn't come back without a new pair of water shoes, not snogs, but real water shoes purchased from athletic stores in town.

Many children love to go away to camp or do camping in a tent. They love to be out in nature, to explore. They love campfires and sleeping in sleeping bags. They love lanterns, observing weird bugs they don't see at home, and lifting rocks to search for salamanders in the moist earth beneath.

Frank spent a good part of his day raking up some of the rocks to make our swimming area more sandy. I tried the raking once; it was harder than it looked. Frank always makes things look easier to do than they really are. Anyway, I didn't really want the rocks raked up. I didn't want to neaten the area or make it pristine. I wanted the camp area to remain wild. The wild and wide open spaces are what I crave. Without the rocks and the strands of grass in the lake where sand colored fish can hide, what would we have to look at through our goggles?

We lit the woodstove on early mornings and sometimes before bed if there was a chill in the air. I loved to hear the crackle of the fire as logs burned and fell from where Frank laid them in the stove. And oh, how I loved the smell of a burning wood fire. It was comforting and homey. It was clean smelling. I dragged my rocking chair near the woodstove, pulled on a pair of wool socks as slippers, and grabbed one of the books I brought to camp. Inevitably, until he became too big, Ben would come sit in my lap, quietly, his head resting back against my chest.

And then it was bedtime for Ben. When he was young, after I read a few picture books to him, he would lay down willingly on his camp bed, lifting his pajama top with his skinny arms so I would rub his back. He would roll down deep into the center of the mattress, where it bowed in the middle, with Piggy snuggled under one arm and Blankie squeezed into the palm of one hand, his fingers in his mouth. From his nightlight, I could see how much his hair had bleached blond that summer, tousled on his pillow and his face a soft, golden tan. His sleep would always come quickly. His brow unfurrowed, he was far away; deeply and peacefully sleeping.

CHAPTER 21

Fall

Then came fall. Another summer season at camp had come and gone. Soon the trees that lined the lake would turn bright red, orange, yellow. Leaves would drop into the lake and float along with the current like tiny, fairy boats. The air changed and cooled; I could feel and smell that it was fall air, no longer summer air. The lake quieted as residents packed up, closed up, and headed back to their homes. The college students came to crew on the lake the last week of August each year. I loved to watch them crewing.

The boats skimmed across the top of the water without making a sound and barely a ripple behind them. The students, boys and girls, slid rhythmically forward and back, absolutely in sync with one another's rowing. When I saw the crewing, I knew it was fall. It was back to school — a new grade, a new year, a new season of my boys' lives.

Frank always drove the borrowed truck home, pulling the aluminum boat on its trailer filled with our gear. I lingered and always left the camp last. I'd get a bit nostalgic when I headed my car up the camp road for the final time of the season, and I always looked back one more time. Involuntarily, I sighed, the last wisp of my contentment slipping out of me. The boys put on their iPod ear buds and didn't look back, only forward, anxious to get home to their rooms and their friends.

And me? Well, I always looked back through my rearview mirror until the camp was no longer in sight. I was capturing it in my mind, never knowing when it all may be taken away. Perhaps I always had a premonition it would happen again; I take nothing for granted.

I was grateful to have had another wonderful summer vacation and I would never forget each year's memories. I observed the boys through my mirror, looking so different with each passing year. I looked back at the camp and the woods. My essential self smiled and drove homeward feeling relaxed and content and trying so hard to hold on to that feeling forevermore.

Made in the USA
Charleston, SC
09 June 2011